FOR KEBEDE ABAYE

PHOTO CREDIT: LEW MERMELSTEIN

COVER DESIGN: JODY SUGRUE

ISBN: 978-1-09-554739-7

TABLE OF CONTENTS

Author's Note

Everyone depicted in these stories is real. However, I have changed the names of many individuals either out of privacy concerns or to avoid confusing the reader where two or more people shared the same name or had very similar names. I thought it would be difficult enough for a non-Amharic speaking reader to keep track of so many characters with their Amharic names. To keep track of several characters with the same or very similar names would be asking too much.

Again, out of concern for the reader, I have tried to keep to a minimum the use of Amharic words. But several seemed unavoidable. Each is defined at least once in the text but for the reader's convenience I list them here as well.

Birr – An Ethiopian dollar

Chis-chis – Army ants

Doro Wat – Ethiopian chicken stew

Gabi – A cotton shawl worn about the shoulders or over the head

Gorsha – Placing food in another's mouth, out of respect or affection

Injera – flat, flexible bread made of fermented dough

Tej – Ethiopian mead, or honey wine

Tej bet – A bar where tej is served

Tela – A fermented, alcoholic grain-based drink

Wat – Any of many traditional Ethiopian stews

Finally, I should note that this is not intended to be a description of a typical Ethiopian ethnic group or community. Ethiopia is both modern and ancient. It is exceedingly diverse in language, ethnicity, culture and economic activity. This is about my experiences and those of my friends in one village at a specific time in its life, my life, and theirs.

WELCOME TO WAJIFO

My first night in Wajifo a snake killed my next door neighbor.

Evening had just turned into night. The snake had worked its way into the thatch roof of the man's house. Over the insistent clamor of night insects, I heard him shout, "Snake! Snake!" Whether he called out before it bit him or after, I'll never know. At any rate, the snake bit him in the neck. There was a great rush to help - farmers converging on the house through the brush, a confusion of waving, flaming torches and a flashlight or two, a desperate search for the snake. The farmers maneuvered clumsily in the house, trying to avoid the snake's strike. Machetes and clubs tore into the thatch. There was a lot of shouting – "There it is! Watch out! Careful! Kill it! Kill it!"

It didn't take long. A few very intense moments and the snake was dead, stretched out on the dirt floor of the house. The would-be rescuers milled about, exchanging grim looks of relief and satisfaction, not saying much, one of them taking a last tension releasing whack or two at the snake, as the adrenaline level receded. Others tended to my stricken neighbor. He was inert by the time the snake was dead and was gone himself soon after.

I can't recall his name; we'd never met. He was thin, maybe forty years old, and I watched him take his last breath. The suddenness and swiftness of his death made a deep impression. I was on guard for snakes from then on and was suddenly and explicitly aware that I'd chosen to settle in a

1

place unlike anywhere else I'd ever lived, specifically a village in the southern Ethiopian province of Gemu Gofa.

I had arrived there in 1969 as an American Peace Corps Volunteer, committed to a two-year assignment, which ultimately stretched into four-and-a-half years. I'd wanted a change. Open to just about any new experience, I wanted to learn to see the world from a different perspective.

Abroad, the United States was waging a pointless war in Vietnam. Domestically, the civil rights movement was having incremental success, but this was punctuated by the riots and assassinations that marked that period. The women's liberation movement was starting to gain traction but meeting strong resistance from male-dominated political and social institutions. The political leadership of the U.S., rather than embracing and guiding positive change, was appealing to bigotry and fear to secure its position. The Peace Corps seemed like an interesting, worthwhile, and exciting opportunity to get away.

Wajifo, where I'd come to live from Connecticut, was a small village shaded by acacia trees and bordered by a river to the north and a seasonal stream, most often a dry wash, to the south. The village was about an hour's walk, by very gradual descent, to the humid shore of Lake Abaya, one of the Great Rift Valley lakes.

Lake Abaya was home to hippos, crocodiles and other wildlife and fish, including the huge Nile Perch. Lions frequented the surrounding forest, especially to the west and up over the wall of the Valley. They were also surprisingly frequent visitors to the village itself, usually at night. The call "Lion, lion whooo" served as a village-wide warning system that one of the big cats was passing through.

Small monkeys could occasionally be seen in Wajifo, baboons lived nearby in large numbers, snakes were numerous and often dangerous, and hyenas were heard in the woods most nights. But it was the insects, in their varied millions, that dominated the night with their cacophonous calls and inscrutable nocturnal conversations.

Wajifo was a community of farm families who had been resettled from the Merhabete region of Ethiopia's cool north central highlands to the hot floor of the Rift Valley in the south as part of a government program to reduce land pressure from overpopulation in the north and increase agricultural production in the south.

The settlers called themselves the Merhabete after their homeland. They were a branch of the politically dominant Amhara ethnic group whose language, Amharic, was also the official national language. At the peak of the resettlement program there were about three hundred Merhabete residents in Wajifo, including settlers, spouses and children.

The Merhabete had a reputation for being aggressive and argumentative. They were proud and hardworking, confident, tough and not given to capitulation when faced with a challenge.

The Merhabete claimed that during the 1935-1941 Italian occupation of Ethiopia they had stationed a man with a rifle in a tree in case an Italian plane ever flew close enough to take a shot at. They did this for about four years until, finally, as the Italians retreated, some hapless Italian pilot came too close to the tree and the Merhabete rifleman on duty shot him down. They took pride in this story. True or not, it fit nicely with their self-image as a people. However, despite these aggressive tendencies, they displayed the same love of family, friends, and community as any other people.

The indigenous people of Wajifo and the surrounding area were the Gemu. They were distinct ethnically, linguistically and behaviorally from the Merhabete. The Gemu were generally accommodating and conflict averse. They seemed less interested in making history than in just getting through the day. This character trait was likely what allowed them to coexist peacefully with the resettled and generally more assertive Merhabete even though the Merehabete were resettled in the Gemu's home province of Gemu Gofa.

Housing in the village was a mix of traditional Merhabete architecture (slanted, thatched roofs with walls made of branches) and the houses built as part of the resettlement program (tin roofs with walls made of eucalyptus poles and branches). Both styles had dirt floors. Not surprisingly, the steep, traditional thatched roofs shed water more effectively than the tin roofs, which tended to have multiple leaks from nail holes and made conversation nearly impossible during a rainstorm.

My house, which also served as the community development center, had a tin roof. It had no interior doors but was

4

divided into three rooms by bamboo matting walls – two small rooms and one larger one. I used one small room for my bed, and the larger room for receiving company. The third room's purpose fluctuated over time between a guest room and a storage area.

There was no electricity or running water in Wajifo. During the dry season, the trees provided a cooling canopy for most of the village. People cooked by balancing a pot on three rocks positioned on the ground in the house and kept the coals of their cooking fires going around the clock.

The only permanent place of business, aside from the grinding mill, was Mohammed's little shop which was across the main road. It opened during my second year in Wajifo and sold matches, candy, cloth and, of course, Coca Cola. Although not adopted by everyone, the matches were especially helpful to the Merhabete since they took some of the pressure off the need to keep the coals of their cooking fires going day and night.

Over my four years in Wajifo, I saw the village change. When I arrived there was no marketplace to speak of, no businesses, no people other than the Merhabete and the Gemu. Social life was quiet. Farmers, their wives, and maybe a guest or two sat around the cooking fire or a small table with a homemade kerosene lamp, a *gabi* (light cotton shawl) thrown across their shoulders or in cool weather over their heads, and talked about events of the day.

Eventually, during my fourth year, a bridge was built over the river and the construction attracted day laborers, some of whom stayed on in the village. Beer came with them, loud music over the radio, cigarettes, and inevitably a few prostitutes. Theft began to be a problem and fights would occasionally break out in the market which had become rather large and attracted a major crowd every Tuesday, market day.

This encroaching urbanization compounded the legal issues threatening the Merhabete's land titles. Despite all this, the Merhabete managed to maintain a separate and distinctive identity, at least while I was there, but change was definitely coming.

All of this would come later however. That first night in Wajifo, as I cautiously stretched out under my blanket, my eyes searching the shadows for snakes, all I could think was: What the hell am I doing here?

St. Michael's Day Feast

Before getting to Wajifo but after I'd been in Ethiopia about
three weeks studying the Amharic language and undergoing
cross-cultural training, the Peace Corps Volunteer trainees
in my group were sent out, alone, to various places around
the country for a few days. The goal was to practice our
newly, barely acquired Amharic and to have whatever cross-
cultural experiences might present themselves.

I landed in a small village in the highlands about two
hundred kilometers north of Addis Abeba. Two local
Ethiopian community development workers were there, and
I attached myself to them. They were kind enough to put me
up in the small building they used as an office. I'd arrived in
the late afternoon and the next day was a holiday, Saint
Michael's Day. Most of the village was going up to the top
of a nearby mountain for the celebration and the community
development workers invited me along. We were to leave at
sunrise, and there would be mules to ride.

I was ready, eager, and waiting outside as the sky lightened.
There might have been some coffee but certainly nothing to
eat and we were off, up the trail to the mountaintop. The
walking was pleasant in the thin, cool morning air of the
mountains, the smell of eucalyptus invigorating. I walked
most of the way but tried riding a mule as the morning
progressed, the climb became steeper and the radiation of
the high-altitude sun stronger.

At mid-morning, we arrived on the mountaintop where the
air was breezy but the sun fierce. A large, good humored,

holiday crowd milled about an open grassy area. The religious ceremonies marking the day were elaborate and colorful. Most eye catching were the bright hues of the Orthodox priests' clothing and parasols. I felt privileged to be witnessing an ancient religious ceremony, a manifestation of Ethiopia's rich cultural traditions. The chanting of prayers in the ecclesiastical language Geez, the rhythmic movements of the priests, everything unfolding around me enhanced the immediacy of my sense of place and time, sharpened perhaps by the menthol aroma of eucalyptus. I tried to not miss anything, although I understood little.

Eventually, however, I was hungry. Very hungry. And thirsty. I had always had a fast metabolism. Three meals a day was my minimum requirement. To miss two consecutive meals was to abandon hope. No food vendors were in sight and by mid-afternoon my interest in the ceremonies had waned and I'd retreated to the shade of a large eucalyptus to think about food and drink, and to hope that both would somehow soon appear.

At the cusp of despair, I was delighted when one of the community development workers collected me and we moved toward a large, round, thatched roof building where he said we would get something to eat before heading back down the mountain. My grasp of the language was tenuous but my sense was that we were guests of the community hosting the ceremonies.

As we approached and entered the building, goats were being slaughtered by the entrance. They were hung upside down from a tree branch and their throats were cut. Two were being butchered, a couple of others were in the process of being slaughtered with much kicking and strangled rasping sounds as their blood splashed out onto the ground. Others, nearby the tree, were bleating loudly in protest. None of this stimulated my appetite but it didn't need stimulation. I was ravenous.

It was blessedly cool in the building. The earthen floor was plastered with mud and cow dung, the roof thick thatch, and the walls were branches plastered with mud. The furniture consisted of long, low benches made of split logs, flat side up, stabilized with rocks, arranged along the curving wall. In front of the benches were tables, thick slabs of wood supported in the same way as the benches, so that sitting on a bench one would be in nearly a squatting position, leaning forward between the knees to reach whatever food might be on the table.

I sat squeezed between two strangers, middle-aged men, and was surprised to notice that just behind me and slightly to the right was a cow, tethered to the wall. When I stretched backward my elbow would touch the cow's rump. Along with much else I experienced that day, this arrangement was new to me. We didn't do this back in Connecticut.

As I pondered possible reasons for the cow being in the house, we were all handed dried, hollow gourds and drinks were soon poured into the gourds from large clay jugs. The drink was *tela,* a mildly alcoholic drink sometimes compared to beer because both are made from fermented grain. But *tela* neither looks nor tastes anything like beer. And although I later came to love it, that day *tela* was brand new to me, a pale amber-colored, sour-tasting drink with little things

9

floating in it. But I was very thirsty and this was the available drink so – cheers!

Soon, food began to arrive - warm, raw goat meat, carried to the table in large baskets sodden with blood. The meat was deposited in neat but generous piles that three, maybe four diners, crowded closely together, could share. Spaced conveniently along the table between the meat piles were small servings of crushed red pepper and coarse salt for dipping. Sharpened knives were made available. Though warm, the meat had not been heated. It had just been carved from the body of a freshly slaughtered goat. It was body temperature. The ragged, rasping, strangled cry of another goat filtered into the house. People began eating, cutting bite size chunks from the meat and popping it into their mouths by hand. My neighbor to the right nudged me. "Eat!" he said, gesturing toward the meat pile directly in front of me.

I thought, this is living tissue. The goat's spirit is still hovering.

My tablemate was eating enthusiastically, a small seep of blood at the corner of his mouth. "Eat!" he gestured again. "What is it? What's the matter? Eat!"

I ate. I ate hurriedly, and as mindlessly as possible. I cut off chunks of warm meat, coated them lavishly with blistering red pepper and salt, stuffed them as far back into my mouth as I could and tried to think diverting thoughts – the names of my childhood neighbors, multiplication tables, anything. I chewed aggressively and washed the meat down as quickly as I could with large gulps of *tela*.

My tablemate nudged me again and gestured for me to open my mouth. As I did he reached over and into my mouth, in past my teeth, where he deposited a generous morsel of meat and smiled, "Eat!" This thoughtful gesture, sharing food in a most direct and personal way, is called a *gorsha*. My neighbor to the left began offering *gorshas* as well.

Just as I'd washed down maybe the fourth or fifth *gorsha* with a long swallow of *tela* the cow behind me urinated forcefully, splattering fresh urine and urine-transported bits of the mud and dung floor onto my bare arm, leg, and neck and even the side of my face. Maybe into my gourd of *tela*. I stared at the gourd, mulling that possibility. Suddenly, the splashing cow urine, the sour, amber-colored drink with the little things floating in it, the warm, living meat, and the harsh, strangled cries of the dying goats became a single, unitary experience in what began to seem a very hot and very crowded room, and my esophagus, wisely I think, elected to shut down. I could chew all I wanted from then on but nothing else would be permitted to pass my tonsils. My digestive tract had had quite enough.

In fact, I think my entire body, my very being had received more than enough stimulation for one day. My memory of the rest of that day is vague. The meal, of course, eventually ended, and I like to believe my leave-taking was gracious, maybe even dignified. As evening descended I rode at least part of the way down the mountain on the mule as I tried to figure out which mode of travel more effectively decreased pressure on my intestinal tract - stumbling in the dark on the uneven ground or bouncing along on the mule. I know for a fact that the night was long and physiologically explosive.

The next morning I was several pounds lighter and desperate for coffee and dry bread.

DECISION TO STAY

By the time I arrived in Wajifo, I'd fallen in love with Ethiopian cuisine. I'd been pleased to learn that the dominant cuisine was not warm, raw goat, which was a delicacy, but *injera* and *wat*. *Injera* is a flat, flexible, almost rubbery bread made from fermented batter, and *wat* is a generally thick stew made from any of a wide variety of meats, legumes, and vegetables, richly flavored with characteristic but diverse combinations of spices. People ate from a round, shared tray, tearing off pieces of *injera* and using them to scoop up the *wat*.

I was still coming to terms with *tela*. Always homemade, it varied considerably in quality from one encounter to another. Reliably better, and stronger, was *tej*, an Ethiopian style mead, or honey wine.

In the end, it was the water that was most problematic.

Early on, I had decided to eat or drink whatever was offered to me. To the extent possible I wanted to live the life of an Ethiopian peasant farmer. I was young, of course, and therefore immortal but this decision introduced me to the intestinal drama of amoebic dysentery. As a result, I had arrived in Wajifo about twenty pounds lighter than I'd weighed when arriving in Ethiopia.

I'd taken the arsenic-based medicine for dysentery but Wajifo's water source was the tea-colored river north of the village so I knew I would keep re-infecting myself even while taking the foul-tasting treatment. It was possible, of course, to treat the river water by boiling it but none of the Wajifo farm families did that and I did not want to turn down every drink offered to me over the coming years. I decided that infections from polluted water were culturally unavoidable and, since the farmers lived with the parasites, I quit the arsenic treatment and learned to live with them too.

A couple of months after my arrival in Wajifo, I decided one evening that it was time to explore this river whose very existence, as water source, made the village possible and whose microscopic wildlife I had adopted as my own. So, the next morning I packed a little food, walked out to the river and headed upstream.

About ten minutes above the village I stopped at what would become my favorite bathing place. A small forested island shaded a shallow pool here. A rather open area of rock spread out behind me, and there was a clear view for a couple of hundred meters down a straight stretch of river below me. I was in no hurry so I sat on a rock midstream and enjoyed just being there.

After no more than two or three minutes I heard the clatter of small hooves on the rock behind me and turned to see a family of wart hogs crossing the rock to drink at the river. The mother noticed me, grunted, and moved her brood of young ones upstream to a safer spot. The little ones were miniatures, apparent clones of the adult so not cute or beautiful but appealing nonetheless.

Pigs can be temperamental so I glanced back from time to time in case the mom decided that she wanted me to move along. But they were polite, respected my space and drifted back into the open woods after hydrating. Moments later a troop of baboons appeared on the river bank downstream. First one adult, then a couple, then the whole troop - babies, young ones, parents, the large older males. The adults kept a careful eye on me while everyone had a drink. Lingering young ones, displaying too much curiosity about me, were swatted, and sent back into the woods. Finally, the entire troop withdrew. I sat there a while longer reflecting on the fact that I was living on the edge of wilderness where interactions with wildlife and genuine solitude were only a stroll away. Then I stood up, stretched, and continued my trek upstream.

The river was rather wide, rocky and straight as it passed the village but it took a sharp turn a few hundred meters upstream and began to narrow. There were a few wide stretches in the river after that but the trend was a narrowing to the point where eventually it flowed through a gorge. The going was steadily uphill but not hard, mostly hopping rock-to-rock, or wading while keeping an eye out for snakes and other wildlife. A breeze blew down the gorge. It was a wild, lonesome, and beautiful setting.

Each turn in the river brought a new vista and a deeper feeling of solitude until eventually, about an hour or so above the village, further progress was blocked by a substantial waterfall pounding down into a wide, deep pool. The rock face of the cliff over which the water tumbled curved forward on both sides of the falls so the effect was that of a large bowl, or an amphitheater.

My hike had to end here because there was no way around or over the waterfall. The walls of the gorge were high, steep, crumbly rock, studded with fossils. Vines dangled down from above. Looking backward, downstream, the boulder-strewn riverbed fell away rather steeply. No sign of human visitors. Just the roar of the water, the vines swaying gently in the breezes, the mist from the waterfall cooling, almost chilling, the air around the pool. It was a magical, primeval place.

I took off my clothes and waded in on the smooth river rocks, then dove into the surprisingly cold water. The chill of the water, I later learned, derived from the fact that the river ran through a steep gorge above the falls, protected from the warming sun virtually from its source to the falls.

After dolphining around in the pool for a while I swam toward the falls. The force of the water kept driving me back but swimming hard and pushing with my feet against the underwater rocks I was able finally to reach the falling water and work myself underneath it. The water pounded down on my shoulders, my head and back as I maneuvered around, clinging precariously to the smooth wet boulders. My goal was to get into the small hollow behind the falls and stand up there on the jumble of rocks that had fallen down from above. Who wouldn't want to do that?

Finally, briefly, there I was, standing up, looking out at the world through the thick distorting lens of falling water, breathing the dank river air, hidden from view, alone in a cool, secret place.

Chill finally drove me back through the falls, across the pool and out to the warm dry rocks at the water's edge where I sat on a boulder in the sun for a while, contemplating the falls, and eating some *injera* and bananas. I stretched out, puffed on a joint and regarded my surroundings. It really was a magnificent setting – a place of shimmering beauty, compositional integrity, and perfect sensual coherence. The only sound the thunder of the falls.

Eventually, it was time to go. I pulled on my clothes, gazed for a few more moments at the falls and then headed down the river with an enhanced sense of life's grace and magic.

It was in this mindset that I came around a bend and sudden movement to the right caught my eye. I froze. Under the spell of the falls, I'd forgotten that lions, snakes, leopards and other animals were part of the landscape here and that I was quite alone. Now, expecting the worst, with my adrenaline rising, I slowly turned my head. There, staring at me from a few meters away, was a greater kudu, a large, regal, heavy-bodied antelope with long spiral horns. Just the two of us and the river.

We made eye contact and for a few moments we regarded each other – I in awe, he judging the threat. We'd both been surprised. Finally, opting for discretion, the kudu bounded smoothly away, with that magnificent grace of large animals in slow motion, up the steep, sparsely wooded riverbank. He paused once or twice to look back then disappeared into the scrubby landscape.

Elated by this unexpected encounter, I relaxed, exhaled, and enjoyed a cooling breeze carrying the scent of the waterfall before continuing to descend the river, hopping rock to rock, still a long way from home. Eventually, however, the setting began to look familiar, the river straightened out as it neared the village, and finally I spotted Merhabete houses at the edge of the village itself. I was home.

That thought entered my head effortlessly but I immediately knew it was true.

I was living in an area rich with wildlife, in a small Ethiopian village among peasant farm families whose material culture was essentially Iron Age, yet whose language, history and social structure was rich, complex and ancient. I was forming genuine friendships among them. These people lived the way most people have lived most places throughout all of human history. This was truly the human condition. And I felt at home.

Although the normal tour of duty for a Peace Corps Volunteer was two years of service, it was possible to extend that time. I decided at that moment that I would stay as long as I could, as long as they'd let me.

ADOPTING BREHANE

There were natural leaders in the community, not elected to any formal position of authority, but looked to for direction and able to sway opinion by argument or often by simply making a decision. Kebede, a farmer in his forties, was one of those, probably the standout. The farmers generally listened to him and followed his advice on issues or projects.

I did too even though it was a running joke that Kebede was not the brightest guy in the village, a fact he would openly acknowledge by rapping his knuckles on his head, smiling, and saying "This is rock." Still, he was greatly admired for his farming skills, his honesty, his hard work, his sincerity and his pragmatism.

His younger brother Bahylu, also a Wajifo farmer, was about my age, easy-going but ready to help out anyone in need, and always ready to share some *tela* with a friend.

Kebede and Bahylu had brought their youngest brother, Brehane, down from Merhabete to Wajifo in order to take advantage of the new primary school. Nobody in the family could read and they thought it about time that somebody could.

Brehane lived with Kebede, who was married and had two young sons and a daughter. Bahylu also did what he could to support Brehane but he was single and just getting by.

Both Kebede and Bahylu would normally bring Brehane with them when either one of them visited me in the evening so Brehane could take advantage of my table and my little homemade kerosene lamps to do his homework. There was no table larger than the tiny one used to hold the dinner tray in Kebede's or Bahylu's house and, in those days, no lamps either. Eventually Brehane began coming over with his friend Tadesa whether an older brother was with him or not. They became a regular presence in my house.

One day Kebede and I were chatting about nothing in particular when he said he wanted to ask me a favor. Since Brehane was spending so much time at my house anyway, since he was a strain on Kebede's household – one more mouth to feed – and Bahylu's single dwelling wasn't suitable, would I consider letting him live with me. He and Bahylu had talked it over and thought this would be best for their brother. The understanding would be that I would cover any school costs, feed him and in general take him on as a family member, a son.

What he was proposing was not really unusual. Many Peace Corps Volunteers provided housing and other support to students who then earned their keep through doing chores, helping with projects, and so forth. What Kebede and Bahylu were proposing was a bit more formal, involved a broader commitment to Brehane's welfare, and the suggestion that he would be like a son was certainly unusual but it was not really a difficult favor to grant. Brehane seemed like a quiet, serious kid and I couldn't see that he would be an imposition. I could let him use the room I'd been using for storage and as a guest room and it would serve him nicely.

So I agreed while pressing the point that Brehane would be a student, he would go to school regularly and not spend his days doing field work. Kebede said that would be fine with him and Bahylu. The goal was to educate a member of their family, and to provide a decent life for Brehane. It would also be handy for me to have someone around who could help out on occasional chores, feed the chickens and rabbits when I was away overnight, and so forth. So Brehane moved in.

The arrangement worked out according to plan for a few weeks until Kebede began stopping Brehane on his way to school and redirecting him to field work alongside himself and Bahylu. To his credit, Bahylu would occasionally intervene, arguing that Brehane was supposed to be a student and that they could get the work done without his help anyway. But Kebede was the family authority figure. Eventually Brehane told me about these disruptions in his studies and I stopped by Kebede's house that evening to share some *tela* and to remind him of our agreement.

I reiterated that our goal was to provide an education for Brehane, that I had taken on responsibility for his brother so that he could become a student. If Brehane would be working on and contributing to the farm instead of going to school, he should be living with Kebede. But if he was going to continue to live with me, he needed to be in school although, of course, I wouldn't mind at all if he helped out on the farm when classes were out.

Kebede, who had no idea how formal schooling worked, the need to attend class regularly in order to keep up, for example, immediately agreed to leave Brehane to advance in school and assured me he was grateful for my taking on responsibility for his younger brother.

We proceeded with that renewed understanding for a couple more weeks until one day when Kebede spotted Brehane kicking a ball around with a group of students on his way home from school and it triggered something in him. Kebede grabbed Brehane by the shirt and began beating him with a club, calling him lazy and worthless. Brehane took several hard hits before breaking away and running back to my place where he showed me the bruises beginning to appear on his face.

Kebede didn't appear that evening so I went looking for him and found him and Bahylu the next morning. Kebede was embarrassed and apologized but I told him we couldn't continue this way. Bahylu nodded in apparent agreement, glancing at his brother but not saying anything.

"Why don't we gather a group of the elders to work out a solution?" I suggested.

This was the traditional way to resolve disputes. For egregious behavior like theft, there were real penalties the elders could impose such as being denied the right to participate in the community's shared herding of cattle, or being denied fire if the offender's cooking fire were to go out. But the elders tended to produce a determination that came close to justice while allowing everyone to live in peace in the village. Wisdom was the dominant theme and virtue of their deliberations.

Once, Tesfaye and Mulugeta, two Wajifo farmers, got into a drunken brawl over a woman. Mulugeta hit Tesfaye in the head with a club, leaving a permanent dent in his temple. Not only did the elders figure out a way for the denter to make amends with the dentee without losing face, but even for their friendship to be restored.

So Kebede quickly agreed to a consultation with the elders. We jointly identified elders we expected to be both understanding and fair, committed ourselves to abide by their ruling whatever it might be, then met with them to explain our predicament. The solution, promptly arrived at, was that Brehane would live with me, as if he were my son. I would be responsible for housing, feeding and, in general, caring for him while supporting his education. Kebede and Bahylu would give up all rights to Brehane's labor while, at the same time, being freed of all responsibility for care of their younger brother. This was essentially the same as our initial, loose agreement but was formal and recognized by the village elders and therefore, locally at least, carried the weight of a legal ruling.

There were no further misunderstandings over Brehane's education or his ability to help his brothers in the field when school was not in session. The brothers and I were pleased with the ruling, glad to have this dispute behind us. In fact, the elders' resolution strengthened my ties with the family. Afterwards, I was expected, and took great pleasure in participating in the celebration of special occasions with the brothers and their extended family, such as breaking the Lenten fast Easter morning. In a way, they adopted me.

IT ATE ONE HUNDRED

One evening a group of farmers were at my house drinking tea and chatting when Mengistu mentioned that many people still believed vehicles were powered by Satan, but some were beginning to catch on to the idea that it was really just petrol. Then Banjaw, my elderly neighbor, said he remembered what it was like before cars were common in Ethiopia.

When Banjaw was very young the first motor vehicles were starting to arrive in Ethiopia.

Once a year the Merhabete people would send representatives down from the mountains to the capital, Addis Abeba, to pay taxes and take care of other official business with the crown. One year, they returned with stories of huge creatures they had encountered in Addis Abeba. They had asked someone what these creatures were called and apparently were told they were "automobiles". What they heard however was "meto bila" which means "it ate one hundred." The Merhabete leaders took this to mean that a meto bila had eaten, or could eat, a hundred people.

There were at least several meto bilas, the men reported, and they moved around Addis Abeba as if they ruled the city. Quick and unpredictable, they could turn, without warning, and be upon their victims in an instant. The meto bilas had eyes all around them and you could look in through the eyes and see the people they'd eaten inside looking out at you helplessly. Once inside, there was nothing anyone could do to save them.

"They looked like this", said Banjaw, placing his arms straight down by his sides, on his face, in his eyes, an expression of sad resignation and forlorn hopelessness.

The meto bilas made a harsh noise, a kind of barking, the men reported, and the city people would run to get out of the way. You had to run or they might eat you too. The meto bilas were taking over the city and not only was nobody doing anything to stop them, the city people were so intimidated that they built special roads for the meto bilas to make it easy for them to get around.

The Merhabete people were shocked and their already deep contempt for city people intensified. What kind of cowards are these city people, they asked each other. Making roads for wild animals? Why don't they kill them? Why don't they stand up for themselves and destroy them? Are they cattle or are they men? Let the meto bilas try to come into Merhabete! Let them try to take over our country! You won't see Merhabete running out of the way or making roads for them. We'll stop them. We'll kill them all.

The Merhabete posted informal guards at likely invasion routes into their land and reminded each other to keep an eye out for any meto bilas unwise enough to invade Merhabete country.

According to Banjaw, some time later a Land Rover came bouncing and groaning up a "road" – it must have been a narrow, tortuous path - into the area where Banjaw's family lived. A gorge dropped off below the path on one side, a bluff overhung it on the other.

The unnatural sound of the machine preceded its arrival, putting people on alert. Then, the meto bila lurched into view and someone sounded the alarm. Men dropped their field work. They ran to pick up spears, heavy axes, machetes, clubs, whatever was at hand, and rushed to confront the unsuspecting meto bila.

When sufficient numbers had gathered, the Merhabete quickly worked out a three-pronged strategy. Then, splitting into groups, the men boldly attacked. Several dropped off the bluff onto the meto bila's back, others ran down the path in front of the meto bila to block its advance, the third group attacked from the rear - cutting off all means of escape.

They swarmed over the meto bila with their heavy iron weapons, assaulting it with unrestrained ferocity, smashing its eyes, ripping through its skin, shouting encouragement to each other, taunting and challenging the meto bila. I don't recall their exact language but it was along the lines of "Really, meto bila? Take that meto bila! Stand up, Merhabete, stand up and fight! Die, meto bila! Die!"

From the bluff above, women trilled encouragement to the attacking men. It was brave and chaotic, loud and wonderful. It was also probably over pretty quickly.

The six people who were in the meto bila tumbled out and began running down the path to escape. The Merhabete ran after them, caught them, and embraced them. "You're safe," they shouted. "You're rescued. We're the Merhabete. The meto bila is finished. It's dead. You're free."

"They were able to save all six," Banjaw smiled, "but as for the others that the meto bila had eaten, well," he shook his head slightly, "nothing could be done for them."

Having reduced the meto bila to rubble, the Merhabete rolled its carcass off the cliff into the gorge, then went to drink *tela* in celebration of their feat and to recount in great detail the individual contribution of each participant to the victory.

Banjaw remembered seeing the remains of the meto bila where it had come to rest. When he was a little boy his father used to point out the bones of the meto bila, down below among the rocks at the bottom of the gorge. "Its bones made good plows. Other tools too", he grinned, appreciating the humor but proud that the Merhabete had stood their ground.

We burst out laughing, clapping our hands together, then sat there smiling in appreciation of the bravery and daring of those Merhabete farmers, all of whom by now had certainly gone to their reward, leaving only this old man's memory as a tenuous link to their daring exploit.

NEW THINGS AND THE MOON

Some new ideas or household items like mirrors, matches and photographs were simple and clear enough not to be associated with Satan. But others were difficult to comprehend, especially in the absence of evidence, which was not always easy to come by in rural Ethiopia. For instance, while some people in the village accepted the fact that vehicles ran on petrol, there were still plenty who remained convinced that they were powered by Satan.

"So, this is where Satan goes in!" Aserati once declared triumphantly when a visiting friend of mine opened the hood of his Jeep to check the oil.

I had the use of a motorcycle for about six months during my third year and was told by several people that they could hear Satan scream as I rode it out onto the main road. Some were also convinced that the small grinding mill that was set up across the road from the settlement was Satan-powered.

One evening, when a few farmers were over at my house, Satan's relationship with the mill came up in conversation. Mengistu, glancing at me for support, responded that that was ridiculous. "The mill runs on petrol, just like Land Rovers and buses," he insisted.

"If that's true then would you be willing to go down to the mill tonight, right now, when it's dark, all by yourself?" one of the other farmers challenged him.

"I don't have any reason to go down there," Mengistu dodged.

The other farmers laughed but Mengistu swallowed his pride and didn't take the dare. I made it clear that I was with Mengistu, he was right about the mill, but it was obvious that he had no inclination to actually visit the mill that night so I didn't push the issue. The farmers exchanged smug smiles.

Another time, a Wajifo school-teacher was covering magnetism and temperatures, with neither a magnet nor thermometer available for demonstration. The teacher did his best, drawing what looked like the letter "U" on the board and next to it what looked like, well, what actually *was* a straight line. The U, he declared, was a *"horshoo maginet,"* the line a *"bar maginet,"* essentially the English names, except for the rolled Amharic "R"s and so suggesting no obvious meaning to the students as an Amharic-based name might have. Both *maginets* were described as pieces of metal that "grabbed" other pieces of metal.

The *"termometer"* was another explanatory challenge. It featured a red line that got longer, went up, when it was hot, shrunk, or went down when it was cold. In the absence of a thermometer, or red chalk, the teacher drew a line on the board with white chalk and shortened it or lengthened it to demonstrate its functions.

About ten mystified students came over to my house after school that day and asked for further explanation. "How can one piece of metal grab another piece of metal? Does it have some kind of hand? And why do people need a red line to tell them whether it's hot or cold? Are they stupid? Or crazy? In our country we can always tell whether it's cold or hot. We don't need a red line."

I did my best to respond but it wasn't easy and I was helped immensely a couple of months later when a visiting American friend happened to have a small magnet with him. It didn't exactly explain magnetism but at least it clarified what a magnet is and does.

Then there was the business of people landing on the moon. Some Merhabete simply didn't believe it. "If people tried to go to the moon God would grab them and throw them back to earth," an older man asserted one evening at Bogali's house.

"The moon is so small anyway there isn't room for people to stand on it," someone else insisted.

Bogali, proud of bearing, conservative and even somewhat rigid at times, was also a generous and welcoming host who liked an evening of stimulating conversation. He turned to me and invited me to comment since it was Americans who claimed to be traveling back and forth to the moon.

"What do you think, Bill?" he asked. "I think it's wonderful if Americans are traveling to the moon. Ethiopia hasn't done that yet. But are you really flying to the moon? Not everyone believes it."

I made the best case I could that it was true. I told them that we had had a president named Kennedy who, around a decade earlier, had set landing on the moon as a national goal. He was young and smart and energetic and he ordered the scientists to make it happen. And they figured out how to do it and they did it. Bogali said he had heard of our president Kennedy. He was a good man, or so he understood. "A shame that he was murdered."

My eyes misted over as I reflected not just on JFK's murder but on the fact that the mystique of the charismatic young American president had even reached Bogali who was illiterate and only recently arrived from the isolated, mountainous region of north central Ethiopia.

Fortunately, I had the chance to make my case a few months later when my friend Bernard visited. Bernard came from a farm family in western Nebraska, had been a Peace Corps Volunteer and was now a member of the Peace Corps staff, a technical advisor to Volunteers and a friend. He lived in Addis Abeba and put me up, put many Volunteers up, whenever we were in town.

Bernard had brought down to Wajifo an electric generator, a projector, and some movies, most notably one on Neil Armstrong and other astronauts landing on the moon.

Several farmers had asked me in the days leading up to the showing just what a moving picture was. How can people in a moving picture move? Does the whole piece of paper move around? Are the moving people like the little people in photographs?

Wait and see, I'd respond. Finally, the day arrived, we hung some sheets on the side of the school as a makeshift screen, night fell and Bernard projected the movie onto the sheets. The early part of the movie focused on the rockets, space capsules, and gadgetry, elements not easy to follow without some previous exposure to space travel. So, competing with the generator, I explained in a loud voice what was happening on the screen.

But then, suddenly, there was Neil Armstrong on the moon.

"He's on the moon?" someone shouted over the sound of the generator.

"Yes, he is," I answered. "He's on the moon."

The audience, a mix of men and women, Merhabete, Gemu, school-teachers and children, really everyone who lived in Wajifo, burst into applause.

Shortly, the astronauts began digging on the lunar surface. "They're preparing the soil," an excited farmer called out and the crowd cheered again.

When the movie ended and the generator was silenced Kebede asked to address the gathering. I called out asking everyone to stay for a few minutes to hear Kebede.

"Brothers and sisters", he addressed the crowd. "Brothers and sisters, please let me say something."

Then, his voice rich with emotion, he asked, "What have we just seen? We are always being insulted and cheated by the rich and the businessmen, and officials. They think they are better and smarter than we are. But who could be stronger, smarter and braver, who could be greater than men who travel to the moon? To the moon!"

He let that thought sink in for a moment. "And what do those great men do as soon as they get to the moon? What do they do? You saw it. We all did! They dig in the soil! They do what we do! They farm! They're farmers!"

I didn't dispute it. The farmers, really all rural people, tended to be looked down upon by the urban and the rich. So, if it was a point of pride with Wajifo farmers that the astronauts were engaging in agriculture, I wasn't about to explain it away.

MULUGETA'S WEDDING

Mulugeta, a Wajifo farmer in his forties, was getting married to a woman from Sodo, a fair sized town about an hour north of Wajifo. Quite a large number of Wajifo farmers and a few of their wives were heading up there for the big day. I was invited as well and I loaned out some of my clothes to farmers who didn't have clothes they thought appropriate for town wear.

I knew the party would run late at night so, after collecting my mail at the post office, I took a room in a hotel. I tossed my bag on the bed and then, with some time to kill before the wedding, I set out to wander around town. Before long, I ran into Tesfaye and Mengistu, two young Wajifo farmers. It was hot on the street so I invited them back to my room to get out of the sun and maybe share a beer, which would be a novelty for them because they mostly drank *tela*.

The hotel wasn't fancy but it was nice for the town and included a restaurant. The rooms, which were $3 a night, were small with bare floors, an overhead bulb, one window without a screen, and no plumbing.

It hadn't occurred to me that inviting a couple of farmers back to my room could cause a problem. But as we arrived at my room with our beers the owner's wife erupted from the back of the restaurant yelling at Mengistu and Tesfaye.

"Get out of here, you filthy people! Dirty slaves, get out!" she shouted at us from across the courtyard. It took me a few moments to realize that her ire was directed at us or, more precisely, at my friends.

"Throw them out," she directed a couple of workers at the hotel.

"Wait a minute," I called back. "They're with me. They're my friends, my guests. We're just having beer in my room." I waved the key to show that I was a legitimate guest.

"Dirty, dirty!" she kept repeating loudly. "Get them out of here."

Mengistu and Tesfaye, looking both angry and embarrassed, started to leave but I stopped them.

"Wait," I said. "This is my room. I invited you."

I turned to the owner's wife. "We're here for a wedding," I tried to explain. "This is my room. I know these people."

But she kept shouting insults and, inevitably, a crowd began to gather.

"Get these dirty farmers out of here," she was yelling. I looked at my friends. Although certainly clean, and dressed in their best clothes, they were obviously from the country. Both wore sandals and though Mengistu had on long pants he'd borrowed from me, Tesfaye was wearing shorts and so was clearly a country guy, not the sort she wanted in her hotel. It was a class thing.

"We'll just go," they said, looking at the ground and starting to head off toward the road.

"Well, I'm not staying here then," I said. We were standing right outside my room so I just grabbed my bag off the bed. I hadn't even unpacked.

"I'm leaving," I yelled angrily at her.

She was keeping her distance. Her staff was hovering between us and her, not enthusiastic about throwing us out, but not eager to disobey orders either.

"You have no right to insult my friends," I continued. "I'm not staying here or eating here anymore! Never!" I was livid.

"What?" she shrieked. "You haven't paid for your room! Pay me what you owe!"

"I didn't sleep here," I started to argue. "I was only here a few minutes."

But that was clearly a hopeless tack to take, so to end my friends' embarrassment, to end the whole sorry encounter I waved the three dollars at her and said, "Here's your money."

"Bring it here," she shouted.

"No fucking way," I mumbled in English, balled up the money, threw it in her direction, and left with Mengistu and Tesfaye.

A crowd had formed and as we tried to pass through, a man from the hotel across the road, a place called Damte's, said, "Come stay at our place."

When I nodded in reply he ran ahead to make arrangements.

Damte met me personally at the entrance. "Anyone can stay here," he said expansively. "Everyone is welcome at Damte's."

I collected my room key, and went to the room, still seething. The fun had gone out of the day and wasn't coming back. I apologized to Tesfaye and Mengistu and they thanked me for defending them.

They had to leave for the wedding and I was soon joined by a fellow Peace Corps Volunteer and friend named Jim, who was stationed in town and had heard about the ruckus. We'd commiserated for only a few minutes when there was a loud knock on the door.

Now what? I opened the door. Waiting on the other side was a soldier, with rifle in hand, saying something I couldn't fully understand. It seemed to relate to paying my bill at the other hotel so I explained that that was taken care of. But my explanation didn't work. Clearly there was more to it. I had to go back to the first hotel under armed guard; my friend Jim came with me.

Back at the hotel there was still a crowd, maybe a couple of dozen people, gathered around the crumbled money, which was still on the ground where I'd thrown it. I was directed by the soldier to pick up the money. I refused.

"It's hers," I said, pointing at the woman.

The crowd was murmuring, but I couldn't read its mood as I explained why the money was on the ground. The orders to pick it up became more insistent. Finally, I heard someone say something about insulting the Emperor. I suddenly realized that given Haile Selassie's picture on the bills, I had insulted the Emperor by throwing them on the ground. This was serious. I immediately stated that I'd not meant to insult the Emperor, and quickly picked up the money and handed it to an officer. This did not end the matter of course. The money was not turned over to the hotel. It had become evidence of my offense.

I was marched off to the police station to appear before a colonel and was asked to explain what had happened. The hotel witch appeared and screamed that I had tried to bring thieves, filthy people, into her hotel and then had shouted insults at the Emperor when she'd objected. At first I argued back but finally lapsed into silence since this only seemed to encourage her.

Fortunately, the screaming also proved tiresome to the colonel and he dismissed her, saying he'd contact her if he needed to hear more.

After her departure the colonel asked again for my version of what had happened. I was asked to do so again. Then again. Finally, the serious, detailed questioning began: Had I thrown the money on the ground before I'd become angry or afterward? Did I normally pay bills by throwing money on the ground? And so on in this vein for at least an hour.

At one point I explained to the colonel that in my country throwing money on the ground was not criminal behavior and I simply hadn't realized it was illegal in Ethiopia. Simple ignorance of the law. He took note but pressed on with the inquiry.

Eventually I was asked if there was someone in town who could vouch for me.

Since I spent almost no time in Sodo I couldn't think of anyone at first. There was Jim, of course, but, as a foreigner, he certainly wouldn't do as a reference.

Finally, I remembered that I'd occasionally exchanged pleasantries with the director of the bank branch in town. Maybe he'd vouch for me. Jim went to the bank, explained the problem, and the manager walked over and generously served as a character witness. I seemed responsible and polite, he said. He understood that I was doing good work with country people down in Wajifo, and felt that I probably simply didn't understand the law. I meant no harm, he was sure.

All this took at least another hour. I suppose it all could have ended quickly if I'd simply offered a bribe but I wasn't about to do that. It was increasingly clear that they didn't know what to do with me. Still, I could sense sympathy in the room shifting in my direction. What had I really done anyway but defend the dignity of a couple of farmers in the face of insults from a prominent, wealthy woman? Virtually everyone in the room had roots in the countryside and no one was rich. So, in a sense, we were all in this together. What to do?

Complicating the situation was the fact that a large crowd of students had gathered outside. A few of them had wormed their way into the hot, crowded room and were passing word back to those outside about what was happening inside. The students, of course, took pride in their identification with the downtrodden of the world and lived for an opportunity to show it. The downtrodden themselves, actual farmers, the Wajifo delegation, were now outside, as well, pacing and angry. A few with machetes and an axe.

Depending on what was happening in the police station, depending at least on what was communicated to the group outside, we could hear through the window occasional outbursts - cheers or angry shouts: "Let him go!" It was getting dark.

Finally, Mengistu, who had worked his way inside spoke up.

"What has this man done that's wrong?" he asked. "He's done nothing wrong. He defended his friends against a bad person."

He paused and took a deep breath. Took in his audience. He was a poor farmer addressing a colonel and a crowd of city people.

"We're all equal. All people are equal," he continued. "The rich and the poor are equal. White people and black people and red people are equal. You and I are equal," he said, facing the colonel.

The indignation was palpable.

"Just a minute," a soldier objected.

"Aren't we all sons of Haile Selassie?" Mengistu added quickly.

"Amen, amen" the group answered. "That's true. Let him speak"

"Because we all are equal we all deserve respect," Mengistu continued. "That means country people and city people.

Look, we farmers raise the food that that woman serves in her hotel - and she thinks she's better than we are? We work with our hands and our heads. She works on her back," an insult intended to be as crudely contemptuous as the insults she had directed at him and Tesfaye.

"And yet," he went on, "only a foreigner, a white man, has defended us against her insults - we who are sons of Haile Selassie and, like everyone else, children of God. The police arrested this man who means no one any harm. They didn't arrest her who insulted us and threw us out of her hotel. He insulted paper. She insulted people. Which is more important? This trial is an insult to Haile Selassie and an insult to us and yet it goes on for hours and she's back in her hotel, comfortable, while the insult to us continues unanswered."

Mengistu started to go and then turned back.

"Besides", he finished, "if she had asked us for money we could have paid for a room."

The reaction was immediate.

"He's right!" the people chorused. "Let the foreigner go."

Cheers erupted outside as the gist of Mengistu's speech was relayed to the crowd. This wasn't turning out so well for the colonel. I wasn't offering bribes, an angry crowd of students and farmers was milling around outside, Mengistu's words were too on target to ignore, and besides the colonel was likely overdue in meeting friends at some bar in town, or maybe he just wanted to go home. And yet, the Emperor had been insulted. It wouldn't do to have it reported up the chain that a foreigner had insulted the Emperor and gone off without penalty.

So, I was directed to return at a future date. I promised to do so and was released.

Mengistu and I were embraced and cheered by the crowd outside and followed out to the main road. I missed the wedding, spent the night at Damte's, and slipped out of town early the next morning.

I returned twice to address lingering concerns. On the first appointed date I was met at the bus stop by some students who escorted me to the police station. I was asked a few inconsequential questions, given a new date and dismissed.

I heard that a few days later a group of students, in a show of naïve bravado, had somehow procured a pistol and gathered in front of the offending hotel shouting insults and insisting the owner's wife come out to face them. She declined, of course, and the students were scattered by the police, but enough was enough.

At my next appointment, I was told they'd contact me if they needed more information to complete the investigation. But apparently they were able to wrap things up without any further help from me.

THE CHAMP

Ethiopian chickens were small and didn't produce many eggs. Due to their size, they didn't produce much meat either. Still, unlike commercially raised chickens that eat prepared food, go their entire lives without ever seeing the sun, and produce bland meat and pale egg yolks, Ethiopian chickens were delicious, having sustained themselves on grass and bugs and whatever else they could scrounge on the ground. Their eggs were delicious for the same reasons, with yolks that were deep orange and flavorful.

To me, they were far superior to "improved breeds" but I had to concede that more eggs and larger chickens would actually be an improvement.

So, I introduced two kinds of exotic chickens to Wajifo: White Leghorn chickens, which were outstanding for their egg production, and Anak chickens, a very large, meaty bird. They both became very popular, especially when crossbred with Ethiopian chickens since the crossbreeds generally showed significantly improved egg production courtesy of the Leghorns, larger size thanks to Anak genes, and the street smarts of the Ethiopian chickens.

Since the improved breeds and the crosses all lived on the ground, except for a few Leghorns purposely kept apart to maintain the purity of the breed, they ate the same bugs and sprouts and so had that wonderful flavor in meat and eggs that made the local chickens such a treat.

The local Ethiopian hens were the best brooders. They would faithfully sit on their eggs until they hatched, then took their parental responsibilities seriously. The Leghorns barely seemed to know what an egg was and the Anak were only marginally better. So I hatched out these "improved breeds" by slipping their eggs under my Ethiopian hens who hatched and raised them as their own.

I either sold fertilized eggs of improved variety chickens to interested farmers, which they would then hatch out under their local hens, or traded the improved or cross bred hens' eggs for local eggs, whatever arrangement suited the farmer best. Some farmers wanted adult chickens and I accommodated them as well.

Perhaps we were starved for entertainment but it was fun to watch a local hen raising a few Anak chicks. They would quickly surpass her in body size so that when she would scratch in the dirt and then start to step back to allow the chicks to rush in and snatch whatever bugs she had uncovered, she would be slammed in a collision of giant baby chicks, a squawking turmoil of feathers and dust. Still, she would dutifully keep working to meet her obligations as a step mother. As far as I know, we never lost a baby chick due to parental neglect by an Ethiopian hen. Losing a step mother to a giant chick smashup seemed more likely, but fortunately our record was clean there as well.

Of all the hens and roosters passing through the project, one rooster stood out. A Leghorn-local cross I named Ashenafe, which translates comfortably as "Champ," he was recklessly, hopelessly, marvelously aggressive. Much more than ruling the roost he wanted to rule the village. He would be pecking the ground surrounded by his harem of hens when far off in the village another rooster would crow. Ashenafe would instantly raise his head and pose for a moment with a "What the hell!" look on his face before dashing off in search of the presumptuous crower. He'd generally track him down too and make it violently clear who was in charge.

One day I was chatting with my neighbor, Goshu , a Merhabete farmer known for his generosity, easy-going nature and infectious laugh. We were sitting on a log outside his house when his rooster saw fit to crow.

"Ashenafe won't like that," I said, only half-joking.

Moments later the Champ himself appeared, located the other rooster, trounced him, crowed triumphantly and then strutted back down the path toward home. Goshu, who had a number of Anak chickens, smiled broadly.

"I want one of those," he said.

"I can't promise that," I said, "but he's probably fathered half the chicks born in Wajifo so just wait and watch for chicks that look like him. Of course they'll come free of charge too."

Not all animals were so easy for Champ to dominate. Once, I took one of the rabbits out of the hutch and put him on the grass outside my house to enjoy some exercise and to feel the ground under his feet. It hadn't occurred to me that

Ashenafe would view him as a rival but he came charging across the yard and flew, talons first, at the rabbit. Luckily, the rabbit easily dodged the attack.

The two circled one another for a while. The rabbit was all loose-limbed and floppy-eared confusion as he danced around Ashenafe, literally running circles around him. Occasionally, the rabbit would stop and approach the rooster, his pink nose twitching, and Ashenafe, confused but willing, extended his beak in reciprocation. Then the Champ would come to his senses and resume his hopeless attack. Eventually, the rabbit looked at me as if asking "Is he serious?" so I put him back in the hutch while Ashenafe triumphantly announced his victory to the village.

Only once, however, did Ashenafe suffer a true defeat, a rout so complete he was incapable of claiming victory.

An American friend, Wendell, was visiting, and we were having coffee in the house when he mentioned that he needed to use the latrine. I pointed it out at the end of my yard but as he stepped out of the house I called out a warning.

"You may want to circle around to get to the latrine because if you go straight past that chicken coop my rooster might attack you. He's done it to me."

"You're not serious," he snorted, and I remembered that Wendell was a farm boy from Iowa. Ceding ground to a rooster must have seemed ridiculous.

"I'm not kidding," I told him, "but suit yourself."

I watched as Wendell strode deliberately toward the latrine. As if the scene had been rehearsed, Ashenafe came charging from the side of the yard and was in the air, talons extended, flying feet first toward my friend. Wendell, startled, swung sideways and extended his foot to block the attacking rooster. Rather than Ashenafe's talons hitting Wendell in the side, his chest collided with the heel of Wendell's shoe. Hard.

My champion rooster dropped to the ground, coughed twice, and then toppled over. Dead.

"You killed my rooster!" I yelled.

"I wonder what killed him," Wendell said.

"You did," I insisted.

"No, I mean was it a ruptured artery, or what?"

"It was your foot."

Undeterred, though marginally apologetic, Wendell, a biology major in college, performed an autopsy and announced the results – a rupture of something. I don't remember and didn't care what internal damage had caused it, only that Ashenafe was dead.

Wendell then prepared Ashenafe for dinner and he and Brehane enjoyed fried chicken. Well, at least Wendell did. Brehane seemed conflicted. I passed. A true Champion deserved a better fate.

ANIMAL RELATIONS

In addition to chickens I kept rabbits and tried promoting them as a protein source in the village but no one wanted to take them on. For one thing they weren't traditional. And, surprisingly, several farmers told me that my rabbits seemed gentle and appealing and that killing them would be too unpleasant. This surprised me because I was struck early on by how cruel the villagers and others in Ethiopia were to animals.

One day, I was at the river with my friend Tamtim. We were sitting on a rock, having a quiet conversation, when a large green lizard appeared from behind a rock and tentatively began to cross the riverbed. Then it seemed to catch sight of us and raced for the other side. Instantly, Tamtim was in pursuit, running. He managed to hit the lizard with a rock just as it dove into a shallow shelter under a boulder.

He kept throwing rocks into the hiding place and swung a long stick under the boulder trying to drive it out. Finally, the injured lizard made a desperate dash for a deeper hole. Tamtim caught it and beat it to death with a heavy stick. He just kept hitting it. Then tossed the body into the brush along the stream bank. It was a beautiful animal.

I was shocked at Tamtim's sudden transformation. I'd always thought of him as a calm and tranquil man. He and his wife, Kedist, were a quiet, gentle couple who seemed most comfortable when by themselves. They were openly in love. In the evening they could be seen sitting on a log together outside their house engaged in conversation and oblivious to whatever may have been going on around them.

"Why did you do that?" I asked, appalled but also genuinely curious.

"What do you mean?"

"I mean why did you kill it? It wasn't bothering us and you're not going to eat it."

He looked at me, apparently as mystified by the question as I was by his action.

"It's dead," he shrugged, as if that answered my question.

This behavior wasn't just directed at reptiles. Being born a donkey seemed a congenital curse. It was common everywhere to see donkeys being kicked and beaten under heavy loads.

Dogs routinely had rocks thrown at them.

One evening as Kebede and I were coming out of Mengistu's house after dinner we found the exit blocked by a dog that had adopted Mengistu as its owner. Mengistu allowed the dog to follow him around and fed it at least something every day. Kebede paused, smiled and said "Watch this" as he swung his foot back for maximum force and delivered a hard kick to the dog's ribs. The dog yelped with surprise and pain, ran off into the night and was promptly killed by a hyena.

Another time Mengistu caught a rat in his house and injured it so it couldn't run away. He then took about fifteen minutes beating it to death with a stick.

I watched for a minute or two then asked, "What are you doing? Why not just kill it? It can't cause any problem now."

"No, it's bad. It should be punished."

"It's an animal. It doesn't know it's causing you any trouble. Just kill it."

"I am killing it. Slowly."

Early one morning a dik-dik, a very small antelope, came into the village, appearing almost tame. It browsed around the school-teacher Habtu's house and he told me he planned to keep it as a pet. But when he got out of school that afternoon he found that one of the farmers, intending to kill and eat the dik-dik later that day, had broken its legs so that it couldn't wander off and left it suffering on the ground outside his house.

Back home this sort of behavior would have been an obstacle to friendship and respect, but in Wajifo it simply became an expected feature of cultural identity. I learned to accept it, as I did amoebic dysentery, out of social necessity. Life was lived close to the edge here and the challenge, and opportunity, was to understand that, accept it and where possible to adopt the Merhabete's coping strategies as one's own, or at least to tolerate them without comment.

They had no illusions that life would be fair or easy, that rewards would be commensurate with effort, that anyone from outside their community was on their side, but they would work and live every day as if life were a natural meritocracy and they were born to succeed. It was impossible not to admire them and to wish them well.

I wished our animal cousins well too but generally kept that to myself. I felt I was exotic enough already.

LITERACY

I wasn't the only recent arrival in Wajifo. Many of the Merhabete were themselves newly arrived from the mountainous north and none had been in Wajifo more than a couple of years. Up to that point, most had spent their lives in a cultural context of extreme traditionalism and isolation from outside ideas and influences.

One evening a few farmers were sipping tea in my house when the subject of reading came up. Maybe someone picked up a book from my table or maybe I mentioned a letter I'd received from the States. I don't remember. But Bogali asked me whether it really was possible to read and write or was it just a trick.

"No, it's real," I said. "People can read. Anyone can learn to read. You just need someone to teach you and you need to practice it."

Bogali nodded. "I've heard that," he said, but it was clear that not everyone in the room agreed.

Zemanuel believed that it was a trick that the priests played on people to appear smarter than everyone else.

"Think about it," he argued. "How could those marks on a piece of paper or in a book mean the same things to different people? There are too many marks. It's not Amharic anyway so nobody knows what the priests are saying."

"Wait," Mengistu responded. "What about letters that people send, that they write to each other? That's in Amharic. People write and send letters, and other people read them. I can't read but that doesn't seem like a trick."

"Letters? I don't know about letters," Zemanuel admitted, "but I don't see how it's possible." He was pretty certain that he was on solid ground and most of the others, not all, seemed to be with him. "It's a trick. I don't how they do it but they do."

A discussion ensued and a consensus emerged that reading was not something that reasonable people should just accept as fact.

Finally, Asfaw, a quiet, thoughtful member of the Gemu community, spoke up.

"People can write their thoughts on a piece of paper and send it to someone else and the other person really can read the letter, or have someone read it to him, and he really can know what the person who wrote the letter wants to say, what he thinks about something. I can do it. So can Bill."

Asfaw had a twelfth grade education so was fluent in English, the language of instruction in the upper grades in Ethiopia. Although he had no formal leadership role in the Gemu community, his views were generally listened to with respect because of his educational accomplishments and because he was calm, patient, and respectful of the views of others. He was liked and admired by the Merhabete and moved comfortably between both communities. I liked him for his low key confidence and easy sense of humor.

Yet, despite his credibility, Asfaw's intervention on the subject of reading halted the discussion for only a moment.

Then Aserati leaned forward, looked Asfaw full in the face, and said with some heat in his voice, "Do you mean to say that someone can write words on a piece of paper and someone else can look at the paper and know what the words are – without talking to the person who wrote them?"

"Or being told by someone else who knows?" Bogali quickly added.

"Yes," said Asfaw. "That's what I'm saying."

"I don't believe it," Aserati said with an air of finality.

"Look," Asfaw continued, "That's what reading is. The priests play tricks. I'm not saying that they don't. But reading isn't a trick. They teach it in schools. A lot of people can read. As I said, I can read. Bill can read."

"Well, he's a *ferenge* (a foreigner) . . ." someone mumbled enigmatically. Asfaw and I looked at each other and shrugged.

"Alright," Aserati persisted, "if that's true, then if one of us tells Asfaw a word to write on a piece of paper, when Bill is over by the door, then Bill should be able to read the word when we give the paper to him. Without you saying anything to him, Asfaw. Is that right?"

"That's right," Asfaw and I said simultaneously.

The group stared at us expectantly. The fact that we'd responded so emphatically, left ourselves no wiggle room, seemed to sway the room slightly but still only Mengistu seemed truly open to what we'd said and confident we'd be vindicated. As for me, I just hoped they'd pick an easy word.

The test was quickly designed. Aserati would whisper a word to Asfaw while I waited over by the door, my back to the group. Asfaw would write the word down on a piece of paper and Aserati would whisper the word to the next person who would pass it on until everyone except me knew the word. Then I would have to read the word in front of everyone.

I went to my assigned place, turned my back, and even covered my ears. I hoped Asfaw's hand-writing was clear.

Called back to the table, I was handed the paper by Aserati. "Now what's the word?" he asked.

No one moved a muscle. Only the sounds of the insects outside.

"Family," I read carefully.

Hands slapped against foreheads, breath explosively released.

"What?"

"God!"

"How! How is this possible?"

"What a story!"

"They didn't talk to each other! I was watching."

All eyes were on Aserati. Finally, he spoke. "I never said nobody could read. I just didn't understand how. I've never seen it before."

Within moments virtually everyone had adopted this position.

"Look at all the books in Bill's house. And government people are always reading things on market day. Do you mean to say Haile Selassie can't read? Of course he can! Lots of people can read. Now we know how it works."

Asfaw and I smiled at each other, eyebrows up, palms raised.

"Any of you can learn to do this," we said.

"In Amharic?"

"Yes, of course."

The mood turned jovial and there was a lot of good-natured teasing. "I can learn to read," someone said, "but not Zemanuel."

"I could read my name, if I knew how to write it!" Zemanuel shot back.

Everyone expressed at least some interest in learning to read, or at least in learning to write their names so they wouldn't have to use thumbprints, or marks on official documents.

Asfaw and I demonstrated a few letters from the Amharic alphabet, and showed how the letters could be put together to spell a name. Or the word "family."

Amid loud exclamations, the farmers snapped their fingers in excitement at learning something new, a breakthrough in knowledge of life's possibilities.

The group disbanded in a very good mood.

Mengistu told me on the way out, "I'm going to learn how to do this. I'm going to read."

And he did. Over the next few weeks and months he asked me to help with the letters, consulted Asfaw and anyone else he could find who would give him some time and attention. I began picking up booklets and pamphlets on agriculture and short books on folklore that were not hard to find in Sodo. I'd pass them to Mengistu and he'd read them at my house, hunched over the pages, following the text with his finger, mouthing the words under his breath - sometimes smiling, sometimes frowning, but always fully engaged.

"This is wonderful," he'd say. "I wish I'd learned to read years ago when I was a child."

One day, after reading for a while, he told me, "It's like a door has opened for me. When you can read you can know the ideas of people you could never meet. When I couldn't read I only knew the ideas and opinions of people I knew, the people in the village or people I'd meet in the marketplace. Now I can read the ideas of people who live a long way off, and even people who died years ago, people who lived a long time ago. It's like I'm having a conversation with them. And they say wonderful things sometimes and I love the way they say things, the words they use. People write about things I've never thought of before. And sometimes I read things in Amharic that were written in other languages, in foreign languages, so I can know what people in other places think about things. It's amazing. My life is a lot different now that I know how to read. I have new ideas in my head to think about all the time."

I had never thought about literacy in that way before, at least not explicitly. The image of people communicating their ideas and insights across vast distances, language barriers, and generations, made the acts of writing and reading seem suddenly admirable and even heroic in a way I'd never thought of before.

Having been able to read virtually my entire life, I'd taken it for granted. I hadn't had that wonderful insight, the poetic image of thoughtful people communicating with each other across the centuries and around the world, in effect sending their ideas out in a bottle to be discovered and read on whatever shore they happened to wash up.

Years later, reading in Teillard de Chardin's *The Phenomenon of Man* the concept of the "noosphere," that global membrane of conscious thought that connects us all, I was reminded of Mengistu's epiphany and his sense of universal human communication that Chardin's noosphere describes, and what the universal, sometimes brave human quest for knowledge and understanding makes possible.

It was not surprising that Mengistu had an incipient sense of Chardin's concept. He was very bright and quick witted. He was curious about everything and was always open to learning something new and to accepting ideas which challenged conventional wisdom. He believed without question that man had landed on the moon. His wife,

62

Bekelech, was his match in intelligence; her sense of hu
just sparkled, and it was immense fun to spend an evening
chatting over dinner with the two of them.

THE AIRPLANE, A RUBBER BALL, & THE EMPEROR

THE AIRPLANE, A RUBBER BALL, & THE EMPEROR

Ethiopian Airlines flew a DC-3, an old World War II era two engine propeller plane, over the village three days a week. It went south in the morning, north in the afternoon. Six passes overhead every week. It was impossible to miss.

One morning as the plane was just disappearing over the trees on the southbound leg of its trip, a young boy, about 12 years old, came running up the path to my house shouting for me. I hurried around front but before I could respond he pointed at the receding airplane and yelled: "Are there people in that? Are people in that?"

"In that? In the airplane? Yes, of course," I said. "There are people in it. People fly it, that's how it flies. Why?"

"Someone down at the marketplace told me there were people in it but I didn't believe it. I wanted to check with you. I thought he was teasing me."

"No, there definitely are people in it. People make them and fly them. It's an airplane.

"What did you think that was, anyway?" I asked. "What did you think the airplane was? I mean it flies over here six times a week."

"I don't know," he shrugged. "I just guessed it had something to do with the government."

Not only had he not known there were people in the plane, he'd had no thoughts at all about what, if anything, might be in it. In fact, it seemed, he didn't even conceive of it as an object. It was a phenomenon, an event that occurred six times a week. It probably had something to do with the government and if so that was enough to know because if it had to do with the government, it had nothing to do with him.

To me, it was a perfect symbol of the relationship between the government and the governed. The airplane was literally and figuratively over his head - inscrutable, unapproachable, and irrelevant to his life. The word "government" itself was almost synonymous with a distant, uncaring, unhelpful, insubstantial but not entirely benign power, impossible to comprehend or influence and not to be depended on for anything at any time.

The Emperor, of course, was something else altogether.

Hailie Selassie ruled by divine right. King of Kings, Elect of God, and Conquering Lion of the Tribe of Judah were his common honorifics. His name translates to English as Power of the Trinity. Farmers in Wajifo saw him as both real and mystical, a living legend. I was told several times that he could never be assassinated because the bullets would melt in mid-air, such was his power. Some days his face was like the sun, some days like the moon, some days gold, some days silver. But every day he commanded respect and awe.

One day a boy was hitting a small rubber ball with a stick outside my house, bouncing it on the ground with the stick. I had picked up the ball in Sodo on an impulse and just gave it to the first kid I saw when I got home.

An old man walking by saw what was going on, grabbed the stick and began hitting the boy with it. I intervened, stood between the two of them and asked what the problem was. The man had picked up the ball and was examining it closely, reverently.

"He was hitting this," the old man said.

"I know. It's OK," I said. "It's his ball. I gave it to him."

"This was made by Hailie Selassie," the man responded accusingly. "You never disrespect something that was made by His Majesty. You never show disrespect."

"No, it's just a ball," I said, suppressing a smile. "It was made in a factory. It wasn't made by His Majesty. This is something to play with, that's all."

The old man examined the ball closely, skeptically. "How could anyone but Hailie Selassie make something this perfect?"

I figured that he had no idea what a factory was but I also knew from experience that there was nothing to be gained but trouble by questioning or doubting, even implicitly, the dignity, the power, or the perfection of the Emperor.

Luckily, Mengistu had wandered by on his way to the river and took an interest in the conversation. "I've never seen a factory," he acknowledged "but I know they're places where people make things to sell. Things like this ball. This was definitely made in a factory."

Although Mengistu's intervention was not entirely convincing, it created doubt in the old man's head sufficient to induce him to return the ball, which he did. To me. But he glared at the boy and muttered disapprovingly about changing times. It was clear he didn't like them.

I started to give the ball back to the boy, then thought better of it. I really did not want to be accused, again, of insulting the Emperor. There were a few moments of awkward silence before the old man continued on his way.

Mengistu stuck around. I waited until the old man was really gone, out of sight, before handing the ball back to the boy, the three of us staring at the ground. The boy mumbled a barely audible "thank you" and then quietly drifted away, not hitting the ball. Mengistu and I looked at each other.

He'd saved me from possible accusations of imperial heresy. And the boy got to keep the ball.

"Thanks," I nodded. With a small smile and a wave, he continued on down the path toward the river.

Many people in Wajifo found it fascinating to learn that I came from outside the Empire. They had assumed I came from the distant reaches of Haile Selassie's domain since he ruled the known world. This was not a detailed, coherent cosmology but a vague and harmless assumption about who was in charge and how the world worked.

Recognition that I was from a different country altogether, a land completely outside the Emperor's sphere, was somewhat mystifying. It could prompt a smile and a rueful head shake but normally went unchallenged and was generally accepted as true. In fact, once established, it became an interesting topic of conversation. How big was America? How far away? Could one only get there by flying? Did we have the same moon and sun that Ethiopia had? They wanted to know who ruled the place and, once that was established, endless practical questions about how it was actually governed.

After I'd lived in Wajifo a couple of years I was planning a trip to Kenya and Tanzania and mentioned it to a gathering at Mengistu's house one evening.

"What part of His Majesty's Empire is Kenya in?" an older man asked conversationally.

"It's actually outside the Empire," I answered. "It's not part of Ethiopia."

"What do you mean?"

"Well, it's a separate country, south of Ethiopia. It has its own government. It's not ruled by the Emperor."

"Who rules Kenya?"

"Jomo Kenyatta. He's the president of Kenya."

"And he reports to the Emperor?"

"No, actually, he doesn't. It's a separate country. Just like my country is separate."

Mengistu started to join in. "Haile Selassie doesn't rule the world, just Ethiopia. Kenya's not part of Ethiopia. There are a lot of . . . "

"Ethiopia! America! Kenya!" the old man interrupted loudly, counting these countries off on his fingers. He paused. "How many countries are there anyway?"

"There are a lot of countries besides Ethiopia," I answered. "What about Italy? Where do you think the Italians came from?"

"We beat them!" he answered triumphantly, pounding a fist into his palm.

"Well, yes, of course," I'd started to respond when he cut me off.

"I mean His Majesty beat them!" he corrected himself

"Of course he did," I thought it wise to concede. Another royal victory for His Imperial Highness.

NIGHT SCHOOL

Habtu, a school-teacher from Tigre province in northern Ethiopia, and I started a night school for adults, using space at the new primary school. We decided to do it on market day, when the population of the village was largest and when the Gemu would be heavily represented. We'd floated the idea with several of the farmers and virtually everyone expressed enthusiasm, even those who couldn't see themselves actually attending.

Short of stature, Habtu had a big personality. He was energetic, committed to his students and an egalitarian. He was comfortable socializing with farmers, took them seriously and showed respect and genuine interest. He read widely, loved to discuss politics and ideas, and was always willing to make himself available for any project where he could make a contribution.

At first, we both taught in the same classroom, taking turns at the blackboard but soon switched to teaching literacy in one room and numbers and arithmetic in the other. He covered literacy, I handled the numbers although I also tried to make sure everyone in my class knew how to write his name. Although they were invited, no women showed up in either class.

We had to use kerosene lights to light both the blackboard and the classroom and it was not easy. Eventually I was able to get an electric generator donated through the Peace Corps headquarters in Addis Abeba. Another Volunteer, an electrical engineer, installed the generator and the lighting.

This made a world of difference and the novelty of electric light helped increase attendance.

Night school, Habtu assured me, was not at all like his day job, teaching children. For one thing, all the night students were men, farmers, who were used to making up their own minds on things and who were usually ready to debate just about anything but divine revelation. I soon learned he was right.

One night, as I was reviewing the "four times" tables, I got to "four times six is twenty-four" when Hailu, a young Merhabete farmer, objected.

"I don't think so," he interrupted.

"What's that?" I asked.

"Four times six can't be twenty four."

"Why not?"

Hailu stood and began to address the class. "Brothers, Bill says four times six is twenty-four but I don't think that is true."

"Sit down," someone said. "You don't know. What do you know about this?"

Others joined in but Kebede raised his voice. "No, let him have his say. None of us know the right answer. Let's hear what he says."

This sort of exchange happened often.

Hailu started again, and made the case that four times six was actually twenty-two, or twenty-five or whatever he calculated it to be. The rest of the class engaged him or tried to end the discussion, some believing fervently that the speaker had no qualifications whatsoever in this area of inquiry.

I had no real authority to assert when this occurred so I would wait, fidgeting with a piece of chalk, until the discussion had run its course, or, if the debate got too heated, I'd try to settle the issue in a respectful manner. The clatter of spears and machetes deposited against the wall as the students arrived each evening made me hope each disagreement could be concluded peacefully.

Luckily, most often the final consensus was that I was probably on to something, but I respected their initiative in questioning me, and never blindly accepting what they were told.

The fact that class was typically on market day, when the students had likely been drinking *tela* since noon, added yet another dimension.

One young Gemu who didn't speak much Amharic had been a regular attendee and was generally quiet and studious although things didn't seem to come easily to him. Still, he'd been making significant progress writing his name, which required using four letters in the correct order. One night I sat next to him as we went through his name again and he seemed to have forgotten much of what he'd learned, maybe two or three letters of the four.

"What's the matter?" I asked. "You've been doing pretty well with your name."

"I'm drunk," he smiled. Maybe "drunker than usual" would have been more accurate and could have explained his uneven progress over the weeks. Actually, market day drunkenness probably explained the shaky progress of many of our students.

Still, progress was made by most of them over the nine-month life of our little program. Then the Ministry of Education decided that it just wasn't appropriate and we were ordered, reluctantly, by the generally supportive school principal, to stop using the school for educational purposes.

ANOTHER SNAKE

There was a disturbance outside by my rabbit hutch, which stood against the back of my house. I heard a lot of stamping and moving around. This had happened before but when I'd wandered out to investigate, I'd seen nothing. When I checked this time, however, a young rabbit was dead. I didn't see any signs of violence but the other rabbits were obviously excited and stressed.

I mentioned this to a boy, Tadesa, Brehane's friend, who came down the path a few minutes later, and he told me he'd seen a big snake nosing around my hutch a little earlier when I'd been down by the river. Tadesa had thrown a rock and then swung a long stick at the snake, intending to scare it off. To his surprise, rather than trying to escape, the snake had quickly dropped to the ground and come after him.

This was totally unexpected. Tadesa ran back the way he'd come and didn't turn around until it felt safe. I thanked him for coming back to warn me about the snake and told him he'd done the right thing by running away.

"I've got one dead rabbit but the rest are OK and you're alive," I told him. "This is better than having all the rabbits alive but one dead Tadesa, don't you think?"

"Or all the rabbits dead and one dead Tadesa," he laughed.

As Tadesa left, I realized that I had a serious snake problem and not much time to figure out how to deal with it.

I waited quietly in the house for a few minutes, until I heard the rabbits stamping excitedly in the hutch again. Then, without a particular plan in mind, I grabbed a spear and a shovel from the house and rushed back to the hutch.

The snake was very big and it was right in front of me, supporting itself around one leg of the hutch, with its head inside a compartment housing a mother rabbit and her litter. The snake was moving inside and the rabbits were stamping frantically, stuck in a small space with no way to hide or escape. Not trusting my ability to impale the snake with a spear, I used the spear's shaft to repeatedly hit the snake's body as close to the head as I could get.

The snake was suddenly on the ground and moving towards me faster than I thought possible. There was neither time nor space to turn and run. Out of necessity, I was now as committed to killing the snake as it seemed it was to killing me.

The most immediate step was to stop the snake. I thrust the shovel down, pinning the snake with the shovel blade, while instinctively pulling my feet backward. I pressed down on the snake's back as hard as I could with both hands on the shovel while the snake struggled hard to close the three or four-foot gap between us. Realizing I couldn't hold it off forever, I tried to keep it pinned down by the shovel with my left hand and to spear it with my right but it inched forward without the pressure of both hands.

It occurred to me, desperately and irrationally, to try to cut the snake in two by pressing as hard as I could with the shovel but that proved impossible. Sweat was pouring into my eyes, my arms were quickly tiring, and the snake was glaring up at me while it tried with equal desperation to reach me. Time was not on my side, so I did what I should have done first, what all villagers did under similar circumstances. I yelled "Snake! Snake!" as loudly as I could, careful not to let the effort reduce my pressure on the snake.

I'll always be grateful to Aserati for hearing my voice and running over with a spear. I began to think this could end well.

Aserati quickly sized up the situation and tried to spear the snake through the head. It evaded his efforts but did change tactics, giving up its attack on me and, to my horror, trying to head into my house through one of the many gaps in the wall. Desperate to avoid that alarming scenario, Aserati and I doubled our efforts, repeatedly trying to strike the snake in the head. In our frenzy, we bumped into each other, almost tripped, and I loosened my grip on the shovel, allowing the snake to get its head and part of its body into my house.

Aserati ran inside to confront the snake there but it veered quickly out towards me again. In. Out. In. Out. Finally, with much shouting back and forth between us – "Get it! Watch out! It's coming your way!" – Aserati managed to hit the snake's head with the handle of his spear. It came back outside through another gap in the wall but it looked a bit stunned. This time I managed to spear it through the head.

Aserati came out and speared its head a couple more times, pinning it to the ground just to be sure.

We shook our heads at each other in relief and paced back and forth a bit, letting our hearts slow down and the adrenaline abate.

"Big snake," I finally said, still a bit winded.

"Big," Aserati agreed. "Big and very bad."

Later, when I measured it, the snake turned out to be two meters and thirty centimeters long, about seven feet. It had impressive fangs and I wondered what kind of snake it was. It looked like a black mamba to me but I was just remembering a picture I'd seen once in a field guide. Regardless, the mother rabbit was dead, as were several of the young rabbits. Their last moments had certainly been nightmarish. It's an image I've never been able to fully erase.

Banjaw, my elderly neighbor, wandered over, his response to my shouts of "snake" a bit more considered than Aserati's had been.

"This one is really bad," he said gravely. "There's no medicine for this one."

In a society that had folk medicine for just about everything, including rabies, I understood with great clarity that I had literally been staring death in the face from only a few feet away.

"Want some coffee?" I asked Aserati.

"At my house," he answered. "My wife was just making it when you called."

Banjaw took this as a general invitation and was delighted at the prospect of free coffee. He earned his treat by holding forth at length on snake adventures he remembered, or made up on the spot. Aserati and I sipped our coffee. We didn't say much until the third cup, around the time our knees finally stopped shaking.

THE HOLIDAY OF THANKS

I tended to not celebrate "American" holidays. I was different enough as it was and didn't see any point in driving the point home by celebrating holidays no one else in Wajifo acknowledged. I felt that holiday celebrations were basically social occasions or family events anyway and Ethiopian holidays were as good as any other for that purpose, so why not just celebrate along with everyone else? Besides, how does one celebrate a social occasion solo?

But one evening, just after my second *Meskel* – the holiday celebrating the finding of the "true cross" - Kebede asked me about holidays people celebrated where I came from.

I mentioned Easter and Christmas because they were familiar to him, although Christmas was a less significant day in Ethiopia than Easter, at least for the Christians, for whom fasting and abstaining from meat during Lent was widespread and socially expected.

"What else?" he asked. "We should celebrate one of your holidays sometime."

Thanksgiving occurred to me since it was coming up soon, and since it has always been my favorite holiday. "We have the holiday of thanks coming up," I said. "Let's do that one."

"Good. Let's do it," he answered.

80

Actually, the year before an American friend had been visiting on or near Thanksgiving and he thought we should do something so we had a quiet celebration in my house with a couple of neighbors over. But we didn't really present it as a holiday, just a meal at my place. This would be different. I wanted a crowd.

As was the custom, I arranged for several women to make *doro wat* (spicy chicken stew) and *injera* (flat bread). And for others to make *tela*. I bought some honey and asked one woman to make *tej* (mead, or honey wine), not a lot but enough to get things going.

I wanted to serve mutton as well, so Asfaw and I went looking for someone who would sell me a sheep. None of the Merhabete had any for sale but we checked among the Gemu and found a farmer who was willing to sell one to me. We negotiated the price, me speaking Amharic, he speaking Gemu with Asfaw translating both ways. It took a while, with me pointing out the sheep's defects, and him emphasizing its virtues, but we finally settled on the somewhat inflated price of twelve *birr* (Ethiopian dollars, about five U.S.)

I doled out twelve paper dollars into his outstretched hand, counting in Amharic as I went with Asfaw translating and the farmer echoing him in Gemu. Finally, the farmer had all the money and I reached for the rope holding the sheep but he pulled it back in surprise.

He glanced at the pile of paper in his hand. "What am I supposed to do with this," he demanded. "Start a fire?"

He wanted silver. He had tolerated our little ceremony with the pieces of paper but he could not be convinced to turn over a perfectly good sheep for a handful of colored paper. We were a little too far off the road for paper money to do the job. So, back to the village, about an hour's walk, to change the paper for silver fifty-cent pieces at Mohammed's little store, then back to the farmer to take ownership of the sheep.

With the preparation behind us, the holiday finally arrived. As evening came on I had a big fire going out in front of my house. Makeshift benches and tables put together out of boards balanced on rocks or logs or whatever could be made to work were arranged near the fire. I moved my best chair outdoors for Banjaw, the old man who lived next door. A few simple homemade lamps made of glass jars filled with kerosene with a rope wick were scattered around to brighten the tables.

The women I'd asked to prepare food arrived carrying clay pots brimming with *doro wat*, each one telling me to eat hers because it was the best. "Remember, you just eat the *wat* from the pot with the chipped handle."

Or "Mine is a deeper red, don't forget. This is the one you want." And so forth. The mutton had been cooked for hours with onions and peppers in a large metal container – like a small garbage can – over the fire. The *tela* arrived in large clay water jugs and the *tej*, in teapot-style pouring containers. There were stacks of *injera*.

I'd invited about thirty people and, as expected, about forty-five showed up. Everyone got some *tej* to get things under way, then the *injera* was laid down and on it the *doro wat* and mutton. I'd asked two boys to make sure no one ran out of *tela* and they moved up and down the rows pouring *tela* into outstretched mugs, or gourds, or glasses, whatever my guests brought along. The big water jugs weren't much good for pouring so the boys took the spray heads off the spouts of two old-fashioned watering cans I had and used them.

It was a beautiful night, the moon and stars shining brightly overhead, the fire lighting the trunks of the tall acacia trees, the flickering orange of the kerosene lamps, and the hum of conversation evolving into the laughter and shouting of a good time.

I would occasionally start to get up to check on things and was told no, everything's under control. Sit! Eat! The boys were faithful to their *tela* rounds with increasingly loud, but good-humored demands for more *tela* keeping them moving. Women took on the serving of food, and someone would occasionally toss some more wood on the fire.

Eventually, Kebede, who was sitting next to me, took a break from eating, leaned against me and asked what this holiday was about anyway.

So, I told him about the origin of Thanksgiving. The old-fashioned story. The one we all learned in grammar school or from our parents. The good, harmless version. And I played with it a bit to fit the circumstances we found ourselves in.

Why burden the evening with the flip side, I thought, the dark story of the European invasion, the epidemics and massacres. That isn't the theme of Thanksgiving anyway. It's about thanks. The traditional myth is a nice one.

I told him about the people called Pilgrims, who came from a distant land and tried to establish a life for themselves in a new world. They chopped down trees to clear land and plant their crops much like the Merhabete in Gemu Gofa. But this was a new place for them and they needed help. The people who were already there, who spoke different languages and had different customs, much like the Gemu people, saw their plight and helped them, showing the Pilgrims how to work the soil and plant their crops in this unfamiliar place, and providing food for them until their crops came in. Without this help all of them might have died.

Finally, the harvest came in and it was a good one. The Pilgrims had a big feast, and invited their neighbors, to give thanks to God and to their neighbors for their help, the help that made their lives possible in this new place. And the people in our country have remembered that, and we set aside this day every year to give thanks for the good things that we have received and we celebrate it with our families and friends the way we're doing right now here in Wajifo.

Kebede listened intently. When I'd finished he squeezed my knee and said with genuine emotion, "Very good. This is a very good holiday. Do you mind if I tell everyone what this is about?"

I told him I didn't mind at all, that I thought it was a good idea, and Kebede got to his feet. He swayed a bit from the *tej* and *tela*, then caught his balance, took a moment to organize his thoughts, adjusted his *gabi* around his shoulders, and addressed the group:

"Brothers and sisters! Brothers and sisters! Listen to me!"

Conversation and laughter receded. The crowd lapsed into silence and Kebede spoke again. "Bill has just told me what this holiday from his country is about. It's the holiday of thanks and I want to tell you the story."

There were scattered responses:

"Speak."

"Amen."

"Very good.

And there, under the acacia trees, standing there in shorts and sandals, his *gabi* hanging across his shoulders, Kebede told the story of Thanksgiving. The firelight illuminating his strong features, his posture erect, the loud buzz of insects and the whoop of a hyena in the forest, his audience rapt, he spoke of the difficult passage to the new world, the clearing of the forest, the hunger and loneliness of the newcomers, the generosity of their new neighbors, the help of God. And the celebration of this, the thanks for all the good things that happen, for all the help we get, and all the things we are thankful for, with our families and friends, just as we were all doing right now.

When he finished there was a short silence. Then applause. Shouts of Amen, Amen. Thanks to God. Very good.

Kebede sat down.

"Was that right?" he asked.

"Yes, it was right. It was exactly right. And it was good. Very good," I answered, surprised at how moved I was by Kebede's telling of the story and feeling both far from home and right at home simultaneously. And thankful. I felt thankful.

Then Banjaw decided to address the crowd but he was too drunk and by the time he'd struggled to his feet, even he realized that. Glancing back at his chair, he decided that he really couldn't eat anymore either, and since he was now on his feet anyway he may as well go home. Bidding me goodnight, he got as far as the brush separating our houses before calling for help. I went over there, took his elbow and guided him to his house, waited while he peed, got him arranged on his bed and went back to the party.

The hum of conversation had gradually picked up again but the shouts for more *tela* were diminishing. The dramatic high point of the evening had passed and things had turned more reflective and conversational.

Eventually, it was time to call it a night. People came by to express their gratitude and say good night. I thanked those who had helped out and, wishing everyone a goodnight, watched them disappear into the dark.

WATCHING THE FIELDS

Guarding the crops was critical, sometimes fun, and occasionally dangerous.

Farmers took turns watching the fields at night to protect the corn against hippos that would come up from the lake to eat. The men would go out in groups of about five or six, and I joined in from time to time. It was sort of a boys' night out, a camp out. The smell of roasting corn, the flickering light of the orange fire, the good-humored teasing, the stars overhead, the usual sounds of the night, and occasionally a hippo incursion.

When it was time to call it a night we would crawl into a makeshift shelter, maybe chest high and crudely constructed of branches and thorn brush. We'd spread a few leathery cowhides on the ground to keep out the dampness. Then we'd arrange ourselves on the hides, curl up in our *gabis*, and spoon together for the night because it was rather cool and our shelter quite small.

It took some effort, some practice for me to learn to sleep like that – pressed together and really not moving much at all until morning. I'm a restless sleeper but turning over or, worse, going out to pee was disruptive to everyone's sleep. The group would need to re-arrange itself, with sighs and grumbling. So I learned to drink less and stay still and hope for a hippo invasion or some other disruption that would get everyone on his feet and moving around for a while.

I was struck at how the farmers could hear the hippos and other animals despite every indication of deep sleep in the shelter. On my first night of watch, Tamtim heard a column of army ants, called *chis-chis*, moving across the ground in our shelter. These ants were dangerous with their vicious bite and their tendency to attack aggressively and by the hundreds, to swarm whether over a victim or even a stick dropped in their midst. They were called *chis-chis* because of the sound they made when swarming.

Tamtim alerted everyone and we quickly sat up and pulled back out of the way until the column had passed through. Afterwards, we rearranged ourselves on the hides and in a few short minutes everyone was sleeping again. I could still hear the ants' faint "chis, chis" as they encountered small barriers in the night, but it was not a sound that would have pulled me out of deep sleep. We could have been consumed and metabolized by the *chis-chis* if the group had been depending on me to sound the alarm.

Tamtim, I later learned, could allow a column of these ants to pass over his foot without flinching or being bitten. I'd also watched him harvest honey from his bee hive without any protection and not be stung. His technique, he once told me, was simply to remain calm.

When hippos did invade the fields everyone fanned out, yelling and throwing rocks to drive them back toward the lake. It was important to not get too close to the hippos, and certainly never between them and the lake. The goal was just to bother them into leaving and that approach generally worked pretty well.

Eventually, it became more common to build platforms in the trees dotting the fields and use them as sentry towers against baboons during the day, and let them double as anti-hippo towers at night. The platforms, constructed out of small logs and large branches, were not as comfortable as hides on the ground but afforded a broader view on moonlit nights, and they caused fewer concerns about *chis-chis*, snakes and lions.

One night, Bahylu heard what he thought was a hippo just below the tree platform he was sharing with Tamtim. They began yelling and throwing rocks. They hit their target but it turned out to be a lion, a lion who was not amused and who knew where they were. The lion, according to Bahylu and Tamtim, did its best to get up the tree, which had a broad trunk leaning at a sharp angle so it was not impossible to imagine the big cat making it up to their platform where it would have found the two of them frozen in a panicked embrace, not breathing.

Likewise, I spent one sleepless night in a tree, during a watch, when a violent storm hit just after dark. There was lightning and thunder, and the tree swayed in the wind as if trying to uproot itself. The farmers and I covered ourselves with our cowhides to block some of the rain, and folded our *gabis* underneath for cushioning. None of this worked particularly well, of course, and I felt stiff and abused when the rain finally stopped as the sky lightened. Eager to be home, I climbed down and started back toward the village ahead of the others who, wisely as it turned out, lingered in the tree.

The ground was wetter than I'd expected, covered in huge puddles it seemed, and I started trying to step hummock to hummock. My groggy first impression that I was wandering into a low area evaporated when I realized the water was ankle deep and quickly getting deeper. Debris began floating by, catching on stiff grass or brush, twirling around in the current, and continuing on its way. The water was nearing my knees and I felt that disorienting sensation one gets crossing a wide, rapidly moving river where nothing nearby is visually stable, anchoring the scene, and one must keep an eye on the riverbank to maintain balance. But there was no stable riverbank to fasten my eyes on; the firmament was moving.

A snake went by in the broad current, then another. A few small rodents swam by looking out of sorts, and it registered in my tired and foggy brain that I was walking through a flash flood. That realization cleared the cobwebs instantly and I pushed through the water toward the nearest tree that looked climbable, watching for snakes all the while. The water was well above my knees and starting to move me sideways when I finally embraced the trunk, quickly climbed to a safe and sturdy branch, and sat, glad to be in a tree again, until the flood had run its course and had fully receded. Then I came down and went looking for coffee.

WERKENESH

Werkenesh happened to be crossing the river early one afternoon just as it began rising. Maybe she thought she could beat the flood or maybe she didn't realize the water was rising rapidly upstream. At any rate, the water came up in a few seconds and she was suddenly caught in the flood.

Bogali was crossing at the same time. They both made a run for it. As the water caught them he grabbed hold of her hand and tried to pull her with him to safety. But their hands were wet and slippery, footing was precarious and the force of the river overpowering. He stumbled, his grip loosened as he tried to stop his fall. She was yanked loose, screaming, and swept away in an instant.

Bogali made it to shore, banged-up and cut from the rocks tumbling downstream underwater. Several people had seen what happened and tried to follow Werkenesh as she appeared, then disappeared and surfaced again, flailing helplessly against the foaming brown current. But she was moving faster than they could run and was carried along the far shore until she disappeared altogether.

An hour or so later, when the water had dropped, search parties walked along both banks looking for her, hoping she had somehow saved herself. But the group on the far side of the river, rather than the one I was with, found her battered body snagged in the lower branches of a riverside tree. Most of her clothes had been ripped off. I really liked Werkenesh. She was a sweet, kind and pretty young woman, with a cheerful disposition and a melodious laugh. I didn't want to see her like that so I went home and cried.

She was buried before nightfall.

People came by to console her husband, Zemanuel, who was clearly shaken and distraught. Like his wife, Zemanuel was fun to be around, with his wry sense of humor and easy-going manner. But he used to beat her. Everyone could hear it at night. I could never understand the beatings and so his tears at her death struck me as hypocritical while his grief nevertheless seemed utterly sincere. It was a mystery - whether of human nature, cross-cultural understanding, or personal chemistry I couldn't figure out. Still can't. Not that men beating their wives does not occur elsewhere, and not that a wife beater might not cry at her funeral. It was just so out in the open here, so widespread, so socially accepted. And his tears, whatever the cultural norms, just didn't mesh well in my mind with the beatings. Some things just feel intrinsically wrong.

RELIGIOUS IRONIES

While visiting the mission hospital in Sodo one day, I struck up a conversation with one of the missionaries, a Baptist from Kansas who had been there many years. He commented on how hard it was to "bring the Ethiopian to Jesus." I wasn't sympathetic, but I was surprised that he'd even spoken to me so I didn't challenge him. I'd always had the impression that the missionaries I'd met in Ethiopia didn't approve of me or of anyone who was not marketing Jesus.

The missionaries I encountered led such isolated lives, enclosed in their compounds. They needed to get out more and adopt more congenial vices than intolerance and superiority. They needed to go native a bit. Or so I thought.

Anyway, although it didn't bother me that the missionary found it a hard slog to bring Ethiopians – or "the Ethiopian" as he expressed it – to Christianity, it was amusing that he didn't seem to have noticed that this was a largely Christian country. Maybe it was just the wrong brand of Christianity - orthodox, very pre-Reformation and all that. But still, "bring the Ethiopian to Jesus?"

With the exception of Mohammed, who ran the little store, the population of Wajifo was Christian. The Merhabete militantly, proudly so, and the Gemu largely in name. The Gemu appeared to cling, quietly, to traditional beliefs while acknowledging, also quietly, Christian beliefs and important Christian days, but their hearts didn't seem to be in it. The Merhabete took it seriously.

94

This was brought home to me when a visiting American friend killed and cooked a couple of chickens and I invited three farmers over to share our dinner. We were eating and talking happily when Aserati, a Merhabete, casually inquired about who had slaughtered the chickens. "He did," I gestured toward my friend. Aserati immediately spit a mouthful of chicken out onto the floor of my house. And kept spitting until he got it all out, then filled his mouth with water, swirled it around and spit that out too.

"What the hell . . . ?"

"He's not Christian," Aserati explained, pointing at my friend.

"How do you know that?" I asked. No, demanded. "That's good food you just spit out on my floor."

"Well, he's not Christian like us. It's against our custom to eat meat not slaughtered by a Christian."

"Well, it's against my custom to spit good food out on someone's floor."

My elderly neighbor, Banjaw, who had kept eating, was still eating, looked up and observed, "It tastes pretty good to me." The other farmer didn't make a scene but didn't eat any more chicken either.

I finally apologized, of course, for not remembering to honor the Christian custom. Aserati was operating on God's authority. I was merely invoking a common, probably universal rule of human etiquette.

One evening, soon after my conversation with the missionary, I stopped by Bogali's house and the subject of religion came up among the farmers gathered there. What different people believed, how many religions there were, and so on. The light of the cooking fire illuminated our faces as we sat around, cradling glasses of *tela*. Someone asked me what my religion was. I was in my atheist period at that time but couldn't see how that would be helpful, so I mentioned something vague about having been raised "a kind of Christian" and didn't elaborate.

People nodded. "Some people accept Jesus, some don't," Aserati observed.

"And some believe in God but not Jesus," Bogali added.

"Some people don't even know about God," someone chimed in.

"And some people believe in many gods," I said, and everyone looked at me expectantly, disbelieving. "Or they used to," I amended. Still silence. I shrugged and smiled to suggest I was joking and there was a burst of laughter.

"But seriously . . ." someone said and the conversation was back on track. Why get into that one, I thought.

"What religions are there?" Aserati asked. "Let's see, there's Islam. They believe in God but not Jesus."

"But they know about Jesus," someone said.

"But they don't believe in him," he quickly countered and everyone nodded.

"Do they believe in the same God we do?" Tesfaye asked. "I don't think they do."

"They do. They do," others insisted and Tesfaye leaned back and let it go.

"The Jews," Aserati continued. "They believe in God but not in Jesus." He got no argument.

"Then there's the Catholics," Aserati continued and spit on the ground in contempt. "They're bad. Very bad. I don't know what they believe."

Some felt Catholics believed in God but not Jesus, others that they believed in both. Someone said that he thought the Catholics used to believe in God but stopped and so God threw them out of Ethiopia. It remained undecided but they were clearly not loved.

"Then there are the Christians. Us," Aserati concluded the list. "I think that's all the religions."

'Wait," someone said. "What about Mission? That's a religion, isn't it?"

Several people talked at once; some thought it was a religion, others that it was just a hospital.

"But do they believe in God?" Aserati raised his voice. "Do they believe in Jesus?"

"They believe in God but not in Jesus," Bogali said authoritatively.

Others thought they might believe in Jesus, or at least that they respected Jesus, and some that they didn't even believe in God.

I said I thought that Mission accepted Jesus but not in the same way Ethiopian Christians did. But it was clear I was no expert on this topic and the conversation continued.

Finally, Aserati went back through the list of religions. "Well, they're not Islam."

"No, they're not."

"They're not Jews or Catholics."

"No."

"And they're not Christians. We're the Christians. And they're not like us. And that's all the religions so they really don't believe in God or Jesus. So, it's not a religion. Or, if it is, it's different from all the others."

"It is a hospital," Tesfaye shrugged, and that ended the discussion.

THE GEMU BOY

Bernard was visiting with his Jeep pickup truck. We had just crossed the river, heading north one morning when a Gemu man by the side of the road waved frantically and shouted for us to stop. A boy was very sick, he said, dying. Could we take him to the clinic in our truck?

"Where is he?" I asked.

"Not far. I'll show you."

The man squeezed into the cab with us and we left the road, heading in the direction he indicated. It was a short, bumpy drive past a few small clusters of thatch houses, across a dry wash, and through some brush to a group of anxious people headed our way. A couple of men carried the boy on a makeshift stretcher, the parents and relatives, neighbors, and the curious following along. We conferred quickly. They'd thought the boy had died earlier but he'd come back and now they were pressing on hurriedly toward the clinic, maybe two kilometers distant.

I helped the parents and as many others as possible into the back of the pickup, where the stretcher could fit comfortably. I instructed them all to sit down or hold on. I didn't want anyone flying off the back when the truck moved forward. Bernard let the clutch out very slowly and there was a great lurching of passengers backward but no one fell off. Bernard found a comfortable, careful speed and we headed back toward the village and the clinic, rolling

100

down, across and up the other side of the wash, and back through the river, the passengers having caught on to the rhythm of the moving vehicle.

Twice a shrill cry went up, and loud wailing started when the boy seemed to cease breathing. Bernard stopped. I jumped out to check but each time the boy came back to life, the wailing abated, and we continued on, me leaning forward in my seat, muscles tense, willing us to arrive in time, hoping but doubting the boy could be saved. We finally reached the small, one-room clinic. The boy was unloaded, carried inside and placed on a table. Bernard headed back to my place with the pickup but I went in with the parents and the crowd.

The "dresser" (the health care worker staffing the clinic) took a quick look then pulled away from the table, turned toward me and told me the boy was going to die, that it was hopeless. He shrugged.

"Well," I said, "look, do something, give him something. What do you have?"

"Vitamins and antibiotics."

"Well, then why not give him a shot of antibiotics?"

"It's too late. They should have brought him in yesterday or before. They always wait until it's too late."

"I know, but c'mon. Let's try."

"It'll be wasted medicine."

"I'll pay for it."

He regarded me and pursed his lips. "OK, we'll try."

The dresser's manner was neither callous nor stingy. He looked tired and resigned. He was being realistic. But how can you just give up when a child's life is at stake? I'm sure I sounded impatient. Probably naive.

While he prepared the shot, the distraught, milling crowd surrounded the table. The boy was probably about 12 or 13 years old although, due to the slow growth rate of children, he looked to be about ten. I laid my palm on his forehead. He was blazing hot to the touch, seemingly oblivious to everything around him. His eyes were slits and his breath was fast and shallow through tightly clenched teeth covered with foam that bubbled with his breath. He looked small and helpless, naked except for a rag or two partially covering him and a necklace, homemade, to ward off illness and bad luck.

I wondered, briefly, if he was suffering from tetanus, sometimes called lockjaw, because of his clenched teeth. But it really didn't matter.

Break the fever, I thought. I lifted a towel from a nearby hook, and handed it to someone in the crowd. "Soak this in water quickly. Run!"

There was a water barrel outside. The towel came back cool and wet and I spread it over the boy, wondering why does everyone just stand around in despair? You can do something. The dresser injected the antibiotic.

The boy's breath came faster and shallower, then rapidly faded away. The bubbling breath stopped. A cry went up and the wailing started in earnest, the mother beating her chest with her clenched fist.

"Don't go", I remember thinking, maybe saying out loud. And not knowing what else to do, I cleared what I could of the foam from the boy's mouth and tried mouth to mouth resuscitation. It tasted terribly foul and was of course hopeless.

The dresser's hand squeezed my shoulder after a minute, "Let him go," he said. "Let him go. Let his family take him."

"Sometimes this works," I said. "Sometimes . . ."

"Let him go."

I did.

The din and the heat, the odors and the emotion in the small, crowded room were overwhelming. I tried to get rid of the taste of the foam, wiping the inside of my mouth with my shirt, which was soaked in sweat. My eyes were burning.

"It's hard, isn't it?" I said to the dresser. "It's hard when it's children. I hate it when it's children."

He nodded. "Maybe you could take them home in your truck."

"Yes. And thank you."

What a relief to get outside where the air was fresh under the acacias, hot but fresh. I breathed deeply, threw up, and headed home feeling empty and sad, wiping away tears.

I got the pickup and helped the parents and the others aboard making sure they were secure. The small body was carefully loaded. Someone sat in front to show me the way to the family's place. He told me that the boy had only taken sick the day before. I imagined this little boy as an active, well-loved member of his small community. Yesterday.

I had only met him in the final hour of his too-short life yet for some reason I felt a bond with him - maybe because for just that short time I felt he relied on me and I had been unable to come through for him. Or maybe just because it was so fast and so sad. I could still taste the foam from his mouth but he was gone.

We got to the family's place and, after letting everyone off, I stood around for a while reflecting on the dirt floor thatch houses and the small fields of crops nearby. It all seemed so fragile. Bad weather or a distant government edict could erase this little settlement in a season. This is where the boy would be buried before nightfall, here where he'd played and helped out around the house until yesterday.

As it had many times before and would many times again, it struck me that this was pretty much how the vast majority of people have lived throughout most of human history, at least since the invention of agriculture. Hard work, sudden death, very small margin for error. I wondered idly if the sense of humor we humans share and the music we make evolved as survival mechanisms – to distract us from pain and drudgery. Then, with these thoughts in mind, I drove back toward the village.

A few hours later an unfamiliar, older man appeared at my door with a teenager who was carrying a large bunch of bananas. The dead boy's parents had asked the man to express their thanks to Bernard and me for helping them get to the clinic. They wished to pay us for the fuel we'd used. The man had some coins wrapped in a worn bandana. The bananas were a gift.

Bernard and I exchanged a glance and I explained to our visitors that we could not accept money. We hoped that the boy's parents would accept the transportation as a gesture that anyone would make given the tragedy that had befallen them. We would, with gratitude, accept the gift of the bananas. It was very kind of them to send them over.

I gave the man and boy something to drink. They started to leave, turned at the door, bowed to us, and were gone.

THE LEOPARD'S COWHIDE

Sometimes a leopard could be heard at night, its distinctive coughing sound coming from the forest out toward the river. The noise carried well and listening to it one night, Mengistu told me about an attack that occurred in Merhabete country years earlier when a leopard had sprung from a tree onto someone who had been stalking it for some sort of livestock infraction. The man survived but minus most of his scalp. He never looked the same afterward. The leopard survived also.

People respected leopards because, although smaller than lions, they were tough and aggressive if provoked. They were also fast, could climb trees, and were solitary, silent hunters. You couldn't hear them coming as you could a group of lions, or even one lion.

For a few years a leopard lived a short distance above the village. For the most part, the leopard left things alone in the village and people left it alone.

One evening, however, when someone was bringing the cattle back down through the forest to the village a little later than usual, a small cow was taken by the leopard. Since the herder's mere presence had not prevented the attack, there wasn't much else that he could do except guide the rest of the cattle safely home and report what had happened. A great deal of excited talk ensued and the herder got to retell the story several times, adding details, and progressively improving the tale by moving himself considerably closer to the action.

In his first, breathless account he had only heard the attack, saw the brush move but never caught a glimpse of the leopard itself. By later in the evening, however, the story had evolved to the point that he had actually confronted the leopard, stared it down. But still, what else could he have done? The cow was dead and his responsibility was to safely bring the remaining cattle home, which he had successfully done.

It was the Merhabete practice to combine their cattle into one herd during the day, then rotate responsibility for herding them, so it was important to be perceived as diligent in managing and protecting everyone's cattle, lest one lose the right to join his cattle with those of the other members of the community.

His listeners nodded in agreement that the herder had made the right decision. "Very good. You were right. You did the right thing. You did what you could. Once God takes something from us it's best to just let it go and be thankful for what we have."

A couple of days later, Tamtim asked me if I'd like to go with him to see what was left of the cow, and to see if we could find the leopard's den. The cow had been his and he just wanted to see it, probably to confirm that this was in fact what had befallen his property. I didn't think leopards had dens but it was broad daylight and he had no intention of confronting the leopard so I said sure.

We walked up the rather steep dry wash just south of the village for maybe fifteen minutes and then clambered up the high bank on the far side and walked further, parallel to the wash on the edge of the bank. Finally, Tamtim whispered, "It's near here," and we walked more cautiously.

Soon, there were the remains of the cow, pretty much just the hide and some bones, sprawled out on the ground at the mouth of a large hole that slanted away underground into what looked like a short tunnel.

"This is the leopard's den." Tamtim mouthed the words, pointing confidentially at the hole.

We stared at what was left of the cow, the clawed and chewed cowhide. I reflected on the violence behind this spectacle. The fangs. The claws. The strength. The sun beat down. Neither of us moved to examine the hole closely and I began to think this trip might not have been such a terrific idea after all. It seemed very quiet and we both glanced around a little nervously. We looked at each other. Tamtim, slightly built, was armed with a small stick; I had nothing.

"Let's get out of here," we said simultaneously and in a second were airborne, leaping off the edge of the bank and into the wash.

Elbowing each other competitively, we raced for maybe fifty meters, each vying to be furthest from the leopard. Finally, we slowed down, winded and laughing, and walked back to the village feeling lucky, successful, and relieved. We told a few of the farmers what we'd found and a discussion got underway about what was the right posture to adopt toward the leopard on the matter of the cow-hide. Tamtim, a mild mannered man, was inclined to let it go. Over *tela*, however, the consensus of the group became more militant.

"Aren't we the Merhabete? Aren't we the sons of Haile Selassie? Didn't our fathers fight the invaders and drive them away? Are we going to let a wild animal just take one of our cows and keep the skin outside his den? What are we becoming? We're not cattle, we're men. We're Merhabete. Let's at least go get the cowhide and bring it back to the village. Then Tamtim can do whatever he wants with it."

Once started, this kind of talk could have had only one outcome – an expeditionary force would visit the leopard's den and bring back the cowhide. It was a matter of pride. And alcohol. And no time to waste.

So, armed with spears and reinforced with *tela* the group prepared to set out. I was invited along, encouraged to join them since I now knew where the den was and this was going to be fun. But there was no way I was going with these guys, especially in their present condition, to take from a leopard what he almost certainly wanted to keep. No way. These were not leopard hunters, not even hunters and gatherers. They were farmers and they were drunk. I wished them well. I wished the leopard well too but kept that to myself.

The group set off in great spirits. They were five –Mengistu, Tamtim, Getachew, Bahylu, and Tesfaye. We could hear

110

their voices recede as they headed up the wash, the rest of us waiting in a "this we've got to see" frame of mind.

Time went by. Suddenly, a distant shout. Then more shouting, several voices. Then silence for a while and a growing uneasiness in the village. Presently, however we heard voices again, much closer. They did not sound desperate, and moments later Mengistu, Bahylu, and Getachew came running breathlessly into view, laughing, staggering with laughter, and Tesfaye and Tamtim shortly afterward in the same condition. No cowhide and fewer spears than when they'd left.

It seems that they found the den alright and decided that Mengistu and Bahylu would stand guard, pointing their spears at the mouth of the hole in case the leopard was at home. Getachew would keep general watch in case the leopard was out and about and came home while they were there. Tesfaye and Tamtim would put their spears aside, take hold of the hide and move it away from the hole, then they would lift it, carry it off, and all would head back down the wash victoriously. A plan of elegant simplicity.

But as Tesfaye and Tamtim began to get a grip on the badly damaged hide they heard growling in the hole. Mengistu and Bahylu, spears pointed at the hole, urged them to hurry up. This was not so easy, however, given the condition of the hide and the anxiety associated with leaning, unarmed, over the home of an aroused and unfamiliar leopard. The growling grew louder and more threatening. They could see movement in the hole.

The guards were getting jittery. "Hurry! Hurry!"

"We're trying! Where are the spears? Get the spears closer to the hole! You're the guards!"

"What's the matter? Just grab the thing!"

They managed to lift the cowhide a foot or two off the ground.

Suddenly, right in front of them, coming out of the hole, the leopard's head appeared, ears back. Snarling. It seemed very real, huge and invincible.

"It's the leopard!" the guards shouted, dropped their spears, ran for the bank, leaped into the dry wash, and headed for home.

Getachew was gone. "No need to watch out for the leopard," he later shrugged. "We all knew where it was."

That left Tesfaye and Tamtim crouched over the hole, facing the leopard, clutching the leopard's cowhide in their hands, their larcenous intentions clear.

"What kind of . . . ?!? Let's go!"

Dropping the hide, abandoning their spears, they leaped into space and took off after their protectors, already far down the wash.

But all's well that ends well. The farmers got to keep their lives and their health. The leopard got to keep the cowhide and gained the use of four spears.

Back at the village, after the expeditionary force had caught its breath and after the hilarity had died down, the discussion went something like this:

"What kind of people are we becoming? Do we really want the leftovers of a wild animal's meal? We're the Merhabete! We're not scavengers. We're not hyenas. We're men. Let the leopard keep the dirty thing! Who needs it!"

BABOONS

People used to say baboons could count to three. They meant that baboons could keep track of three people guarding a field without getting confused. It was important to keep track because baboons would raid corn fields in broad daylight. If they counted three humans and someone hid or dropped out of sight the baboons were cautious and kept a look-out until the missing human reappeared. More than three people and they lost confidence and their raids lost coherence, or so people said. But when conditions were right the baboons' organization and execution were impressive.

More than once, I watched as a small group of baboons would enter a field at one end and make a noisy show of harvesting corn, calling to each other, brazenly knocking down stalks as they stuffed ears of corn under their arms, waved them in the air and generally dared the humans to do something about it. When the responsible humans would run toward them shouting, throwing sticks and rocks, the intruders would retreat only as quickly as absolutely necessary to avoid contact while loudly protesting the interruption.

Meanwhile, a much larger group, an entire troop, would quickly and quietly enter the opposite end of the field and harvest the corn rapidly, silently, efficiently and profitably. The whole family would show up - big males, adolescents, mothers, babies – and all did their part, carrying away as many ears of corn as possible, as many as their armpits, elbows, hands, and teeth would allow.

It really looked like fun and I pictured them all, the two groups, gathering together later, sitting around, holding an old fashioned corn husking bee, and having a good laugh about who did what, who dropped the most ears and so forth. Nothing dumb about baboons.

One day I arrived at the river at a point near the village and saw an interspecies uproar in progress. People were washing clothes, collecting water, and bathing along a stretch of river overhung on the far side by a bluff maybe ten or twelve feet high. The hillside sloped steeply up from the top of the bluff and was covered in coarse grass, brush, and the occasional scrubby tree.

A troop of baboons had come down the slope, intending to use that stretch of river, and encountered their human cousins already there. It was of course unthinkable that two sets of primates use the same spot at the same time for similar purposes. So, the baboons were encouraging the humans to move along by criticizing them loudly while tearing at the grass and branches of scrub.

Individual baboons would make short rushes down the slope, sometimes right to the edge of the bluff, and throw down handfuls of grass, twigs, branches, even small stones. Their aim was not good but the point was made. They'd quickly retreat back up the slope and others, some singly, sometimes two or three at a time, would make the charge. These were not confident forays. They exuded the blustery air of anxious, adolescent swagger confronted with scary opposition. But still it was a rowdy bunch that did not at all bring to mind the mythical truce at the water hole.

The humans responded more or less in kind, hurling insults, sticks, stones and – less effectively – pretending to point rifles at the baboons by shouldering and aiming relatively straight sticks or, still more hopelessly, by emulating the pulling of triggers with their fingers. You had to imagine the rifle. The iconic question "Can't we all just get along?" was still several decades in the future but my thoughts ran in that direction.

I saw no role I could play there, beyond incremental deepening of the baboons' disgruntlement, so I moved on upstream to a quiet place and went home later by a different path. I'm pretty sure no physical injury was inflicted on either side, and no deeper understanding either.

Another time, I encountered a large troop of baboons while walking to a village about four or five hours distant by foot. It was up over the western rim of the Rift Valley, above Wajifo. I'd crossed the river, climbed up through the large acacias, through the scrub forest and finally was traversing a broad plateau of very tall grass, with thorny trees sparsely spaced. It was pretty lonely.

I'd heard there were wild dogs up here, it seemed like excellent lion habitat, and I was feeling solitary, rather foolishly so, when a dozen meters ahead of me there was a disturbance in the grass just off the path to my right. In a situation like this one is acutely aware of how slow we humans really are, how small our fangs, how ridiculous our claws, how little in general we have in the way of built-in weaponry.

I stopped in mid-stride, stepped back a few paces and tried to judge how far it was, through the tall grass, to the nearest climbable tree. Too far was my guess. I waited. Fully expecting lions, I was profoundly relieved when a couple of baboons appeared, clearly intent on crossing the path.

They seemed as surprised to see me as I was relieved to see them, but still it was not like encountering old friends. This is a tough branch of our primate family and they have really big teeth. I backed up a bit more while they sized me up. I backed up again and the troop began to cross the path. I wanted to appear as accommodating as I could.

A couple of big old males appeared, joined by one or two younger males, and remained on the path, keeping an eye on things, on me. Females came out, mothers clutching, or being clutched by babies. The troop gradually crossed over, all sizes and ages. An occasional juvenile would hang back to take a look at the human and an adult would bark or swat the young one into the grass on the other side of the path. The big males hung around for a few moments after it seemed the entire troop had passed, making sure everyone was safely across. Two laggards did suddenly dash across the path. The males eyed me carefully but with no apparent hostility, and then disappeared into the grass themselves.

I was in no hurry to move on, not wanting to bump into any stragglers, nor in any way to give the impression that I was following the troop. But when I continued my trek it was with admiration and sympathy for this little society of baboons, my primate cousins, operating in a fairly hostile environment but finding what they needed, making do, watching out for each other, getting by.

When, some months later, the Ministry of Agriculture showed up to institute a baboon poisoning program I was not only angry and distressed, I was embarrassed for our species. It was the usual approach. No local planning or consultation, no preliminary studies, just the sudden, impulsive, intrusive gesture of a distant and unconnected bureaucracy.

I could picture it. Someone at a desk in the provincial capital or in Addis Abeba deciding, based on nothing but the availability of the poison, that what the peasant farmers really needed was to get rid of the baboons. Someone's brother-in- law or cousin getting the contract for the poison with provision for a generous kickback, and then the dash around the countryside to get the poison out, with shouted explanations and insults directed at the farmers for not taking care of this problem themselves. No follow-up studies, no safety instructions, no baboon poisoning program again. I'm glad I was in Addis Abeba when it took place.

A couple of weeks later, bathing in the river in my favorite spot, I saw two baboons warily come out of the woods to the river where normally I'd see a dozen or more. They moved slowly, without that alert air that I was accustomed to seeing. They seemed tired, sick, maybe depressed as they shambled back into the woods – or perhaps I was reading too much into this. At any rate I was ashamed for our species and would have apologized if that were possible.

It is true that baboons took corn from the farmers, but certainly not enough to cause famine or even make a big dent in anyone's income. It's also true that humans cleared huge swaths of baboon habitat for agriculture but no wholesale retaliatory slaughter of humans by the baboons ensued. And that's not because the baboons were not organized or didn't have big teeth. They seemed content to impose a corn tax.

I read in Konrad Lorenz's *On Aggression* about a troop of baboons being followed by a leopard, late in the day, along a narrow, precarious hillside path as the troop made its way back to where it would spend the night. There was a lot of nervous glancing back at the leopard as the baboons got closer to what should be their safe place. Suddenly, at some imperceptible signal, two young males dropped back from the troop, climbed onto an overhang above the trail and waited. As the big cat passed beneath them both baboons dropped on it, one fastening its teeth in the leopard's throat, the other into the back of its neck. A ferocious, bloody struggle ensued and when it was over both baboons were dead but so was the leopard.

The writer portrays it as the first observed example of nonhuman idealism in nature – strong, healthy members of the troop sacrificing themselves for the others. It seems like idealism. It certainly is a story of bravery, planning, group identity, and commitment to something larger than oneself. As to the notion that it's the first such example, it may be the first that the observer saw, or at least took note of, but surely this sort of behavior has never been unique to homo sapiens. Scientists' fear of "anthropomorphizing," projecting onto other species attitudes and motivations felt to be unique to humans, has always seemed rather silly to me. Intended to project an image of clear thinking and scientific dispassion, this attitude instead, ironically, seems to project a quietly desperate insistence that we humans are unique, embarrassingly suggestive of the concept, rooted in Judeo-Christianity, that man and only man, is created "in the image and likeness of God."

At any rate, so long as humans cling to the notion that somehow other species are here solely for our use or amusement and that those without utility or entertainment value to humans are simply weeds or pests, we won't have made much progress in seeing ourselves clearly. We didn't create the planet or stock it with biodiversity. We, the other primates, and all the other species just ended up here together. And as for the image and likeness of God business, wildlife biologist George Schaller once observed that if horses have gods they look a lot like horses.

WENJI SUGAR VAN

Wenji Sugar was the biggest and maybe was the only sugar company in Ethiopia. I think it had a monopoly. It was everywhere. Wenji ads appeared wherever there were billboards and its commercials and jingle were familiar to anyone who listened even occasionally to the radio: "In our country, in sport it's football, for food it's *doro wat*, and for sugar – its Wenji! Wenji! Wenji! Wenji!"

To introduce the pleasures of Wenji to the hinterland, a van outfitted with a stove and a speaker system traveled the countryside. It was like the ice cream or hot dog trucks you'd see at a high school athletic event in the U.S., open on one side of the body with a little counter to serve customers. The Wenji van would stop at a village on market day, blast the Wenji theme song over the speaker system, and the driver-attendant would announce that he was giving away free cups of coffee sweetened with Wenji sugar.

One market day the van pulled up in Wajifo. Its sound system was at top volume. Many had never heard of Wenji because they didn't have access to radio and never traveled. Some didn't know what sugar was, confusing it with tea, or not having any idea at all. But everyone understood "free coffee" and the more worldly had heard the Wenji theme song and were intrigued by the arrival of such a celebrity product in our village.

Unfortunately, I was away that day but I was later told that a group gathered, accepted small Styrofoam cups, and responded, more or less, to the request to form a line to

121

receive their free coffee. The more skeptical, especially the Gemu, hung back and watched, waiting to see if this was a trick of some kind. Meanwhile those with Styrofoam in hand marveled at its light weight. Probably no one had absolute faith in the promise of free coffee.

With a good-size crowd gathered, the Wenji man busied himself with coffee preparation.

Suddenly something went wrong in the van. A small flame shot up near the stove. Something had ignited that should not have. The driver casually moved to smother it with a rag. That didn't work and the flame grew higher. Irritated, the driver made a more focused, urgent effort. The fire seemed to spread and the crowd took notice. Increasingly frantic efforts ensued in the van as the crowd began to realize that this wasn't a routine part of the free coffee preparation.

The fire grew, catching on to flammable things near the stove. The Wenji man jumped off the truck, then jumped back on, dousing the fire with water, maybe coffee, to no avail. Soon the fire seemed nearly out of control. The crowd dropped back a bit, staring. Anticipation of free coffee began to turn into the expectation of free entertainment – a van on fire right there in our marketplace.

"Go to the river! Get water!" the Wenji man directed the crowd. He pointed back down the road toward the river. "The truck is burning! Hurry! Run to the river! Bring water! Now! Hurry!"

The farmers and others looked at each other in disbelief. "Run? To the river? Bring water? Why? It's not our truck. Why doesn't he run to the river?"

Besides, whoever ran to the river, maybe half a kilometer away, would miss the unfolding drama – unique in everyone's experience - of watching a Wenji Sugar van burn before their very eyes. This was not to be missed. Even those most skeptical of "free coffee" gathered from all over the marketplace to watch the burning van. I wish I'd been there.

As the Wenji man became more frantic, screaming in desperation, "Water! Water! Run!" the truck was enveloped in flames, the heat driving back spectators who, I was told, pointed out interesting aspects of the spectacle to each other and completely ignored his pleas.

The butane tanks in the little Wenji kitchen exploded, then the gas tank. A stupendous conflagration, a grand finale as the van was consumed in an explosive fury of orange flame, black smoke billowing into the hot air. The crowd murmured in appreciation. The driver kneeled on the ground, beyond hope.

As the flames died down the crowd began to scatter to market day business. The Wenji man stewed in his misery for a time; then someone offered him some *tela*, a little something to eat. He gradually got drawn into market day. No hard feelings on anyone's part about the free coffee offer. He asked anyone who would listen what was he going to do but no one had answers, of course. His life was unimaginable to the farm families of Wajifo and, besides, everyone had problems. He left the next day and eventually a truck showed up and hauled away the remains of the Wenji free coffee van.

The styrofoam cups lived on for a time. A few people tried to sell their cups in the market, others brought them home. I'd see them around the village for a few months. They'd be used to pour water over hands before eating or to serve *tela*. Occasionally someone would look at one wryly and recall the great Wenji van fire to general amusement. Eventually they wore out and disappeared.

SKYLAB

A manned U.S. satellite was due to pass over Ethiopia in a few days' time. I'd read about it in a newspaper during a visit to Addis Abeba. It was Skylab, a large vehicle with a crew of three. The newspaper article described the route it would take, appearing in the southwest and traveling to the northeast, well above the horizon and easily visible.

Back in Wajifo, I mentioned Skylab to just a few farmers, telling them that the satellite would appear soon after dark and that three people would be in it and a few other details. I decided not to make a big deal out of it. Many of the farmers were still rather dubious about this space travel business, despite having seen and applauded astronauts "farming" on the moon, and I didn't see much point in stirring up controversy.

The day came and to my surprise about ten or twelve farmers gathered outside my house in the evening, a little before the appointed time. The group was shyly skeptical, mildly embarrassed at appearing to believe that people were flying around the earth at great altitude, and that anyone could predict when they'd pass overhead. Or even that they would be flying over Ethiopia which, of course, had nothing to do with them.

I had no desire to present any formal explanations but I joined the farmers and, conversationally, described just how far above the earth Skylab was. Because kilometers were not a fully grasped concept, I expressed Skylab's altitude as being equal to the distance between Wajifo and a market town

125

whose name was familiar, a distance everyone knew or had a general sense of anyway. The farmers shook their heads and smiled, shooting glances at each other, suspending disbelief but just barely. I just hoped the thing would show up and that we'd be able to see it clearly.

Suddenly, there it was, just where the newspaper said it would be and right on time. I saw the star that was Skylab float into view above the southwestern horizon. In the first moments, still low in the sky, it was obscured sporadically by the acacia foliage. But as it rose higher it was unmistakably there.

"There it is!" I said, suppressing, or trying to, the excitement that I was surprised to find in my voice. In my chest.

"Where?"

"Right there," I pointed. "It looks like a star. But it's moving."

Immediately, everyone saw it.

"God!"

"How is this . . .?"

"What a story! There are people in that?"

"Yes."

"How many?"

"Three."

"It's so small."

"It's huge. Just very far away."

The group huddled together in excitement, exchanging expletives, shaking heads.

Oblivious, Skylab silently glided higher in the sky, heading northeast. We craned our necks to watch as the astronauts flew almost directly overhead. My eyes misted, surprising me. These are my countrymen, I thought. They're Americans. And despite all my youthful skepticism, my opposition to the Vietnam War, my disgust with racial injustice, and all the other issues of the time that made me angry and impatient with the U.S., I was, in that moment, very proud of my country and felt a strong bond of nationhood with these Americans exploring the frontiers of space. I admired their skill, their daring, their determination to be the best, and their - our - country's technological prowess.

I imagined the flat, business-like American accents of the astronauts, communicating with Houston as they passed over our darkened landscape. Did they have even the slightest sense that they were being observed and quietly cheered on by a group of Ethiopian farmers far below?

Before long, the astronauts were leaving us, slipping down the arc of the sky and into the trees to the northeast. The farmers followed for several steps in the direction that Skylab took, walking as far as my rabbit hutch, their eyes still fixed on the sky. Then, as the satellite really disappeared, they burst into applause. We all stood around for a while afterward, enjoying the afterglow of the shared experience and then the farmers, every one of them, shook my hand, thanking me and congratulating me - congratulating me! – before scattering into the night.

CHRIST STOPPED AT EBOLI

I read Carlo Levi's *Christ Stopped at Eboli* during my time in Wajifo. Despite the title, its theme is not religious. Rather, it's an autobiographical account by a prominent, northern Italian intellectual about his banishment to a small village in the south of Italy, punishment for his outspoken opposition to the Fascist invasion of Ethiopia in 1935 under Benito Mussolini.

To underscore the geographic and cultural isolation of his exile village, he cites the various cultural waves that have washed over the boot of Italy – the Phoenicians, the Etruscans, the Greeks, of course the Romans – each leaving its mark, each influencing whatever followed. But, he observes, none of these "civilizing" forces ever quite reached this isolated place, none extended this far south, not even Christianity. Levi writes, "Even Christ stopped at Eboli," a town to the north of this village.

Levi describes his gradual but steadily growing awareness of the society around him. At first the peasant farmers and their families are like shadows, glimpsed early in the morning heading off to the fields, or at dusk as they returned burdened by farm implements or produce. Gradually, he comes to know them, first as a class of people, then as individuals. He engages and befriends them, visits their homes. He finds them far more appealing and admirable as people than the self-important officials he's forced to interact with as a condition of his exile. He does what he can to be helpful, even bringing his sister, a medical doctor, down from the north to contribute her professional skills to villagers in need.

Levi reflects on the invasion underway in Ethiopia by Italian peasants turned soldiers, an army motivated more by promises of free land than by its national leader's fascist dreams of a glorious, reborn Roman Empire.

It is a thoughtful, reflective and beautifully descriptive book. It appealed to me on several levels. I shared his sense of being an educated foreigner in a society which, though profoundly traditional, is also deeply attractive, peopled with intelligent, generous, humorous, and talented individuals. One sees past the foreignness of the society and meets individuals in all the variety that, taken together, makes each community unique.

The war in Ethiopia plays a supporting role in the book. It's always in the background, much as the Vietnam War was always in the background during my time in Wajifo. The image of Italian soldiers, in Levi's time, armed with modern weapons, attacking Ethiopian villages like the one I was living in, called to mind images of American forces attacking rural villages in Vietnam in my own time. Vivid photos in news magazines of young Americans, my peers, setting fire to grass-roofed huts in Asia made it easy, and appalling, to imagine the terror gripping an Ethiopian village overrun by strange-looking foreign soldiers with horrifying modern weaponry.

The fascination was not so much of the grand scale, the casual unleashing of superior military power by a large industrial nation against a small agricultural society on the far side of the planet. Rather, it was the immediacy of the terror, the paralyzing horror engendered in a specific rural, civilian population by an actual encounter with bizarrely costumed, heavily armed soldiers incapable of meaningful communication. Ignorant and scared young men holding the power of life and death over individuals, and so over that fragile network of human relationships that is the vibrancy of a small community. That, the exercise of that power in terror and in irreversible destruction, that was what was so disturbing for me.

Who were these soldiers, I wondered, particularly with regard to U.S. soldiers in Vietnam. What were they thinking? Did they ever ask why they had allowed themselves to be sent so far from home, why they were in someone else's country killing citizens of that country? Could they conceivably have imagined that these people, these peasant farm families with their fields and animals and with no air force or navy, constituted a threat, a military threat to their country? I thought that these were questions an individual would want to address, and have satisfactory answers to, before allowing himself to be flown half way around the world to kill strangers. And undoubtedly some soldiers did find answers acceptable to them, though one wonders how.

But often the draft was cited as justification for participating in the War. Soldiers had no choice; they were drafted. This struck me as false reasoning. Draftees *did* have a choice, a very difficult choice, but a choice nevertheless. We are, after all, responsible for our own moral judgements. We have no option to maintaining that freedom of choice. It is ours whether we want it or not. It is intrinsic to being human and, as Sartre wrote, the final freedom is the freedom to say no. No to war, no to killing. So, invoking the draft was not just wrong, in my view, but dangerous, because delegating authority over one's moral compass to the government, any government, seems risky behavior for anyone who views himself as a moral being.

The Italian invasion of Ethiopia, on a sociological level, was essentially a grubby struggle for land between two armies, one trying to take land from the other, the invading army being far superior technologically. No such incentive motivated American soldiers in Vietnam. So, what were they doing there?

No reasonable person could make the case that Vietnam was a threat to the United States or to western civilization more broadly. Any argument offered by American leaders seemed inadequate to justify the hundreds of thousands of casualties, the napalm, the extent and the obscenity of the suffering and destruction wrought by our armed forces. And, one must acknowledge, suffered by our armed forces. For me, the war was a continuous source of anger, disgust, and, as an American, embarrassment. I could never explain it to my Ethiopian friends.

One day when I was on the roof of my house patching a leak an Ethiopian Air Force jet fighter streaked overhead at tree top level. Utterly unexpected, it was there a split second after I heard its screaming roar, then was gone. I saw two women carrying water drop to the ground, one breaking her clay water jug. Another jet streaked over, then another. Maybe six or seven in all. It was just the Air Force practicing whatever it was they practiced. No real danger to anyone. But the first jet was definitely frightening and that, taken together with the others, drove home again the sense of helplessness and vulnerability a peasant people must feel when attacked by the modern weaponry of a technologically superior power. The bravery of those who resist, anywhere, is truly awe-inspiring.

SLAVERY

Like so many countries, Ethiopia had had a significant slave trade with well-established trade routes. In general, the darker-skinned southern peoples were victimized by the lighter-skinned northerners. Hailie Selassie outlawed the slave trade early in his rule but it persisted until the Italian occupation when it was largely, but not completely, extinguished. Several ex-slaves lived in Wajifo, people who had been captured when young or who were born into slavery. At least a couple of Merhabete farmers were former slave traders, and one still kept a slave in the village.

The ex-slaves lived among the Merhabete and had land titles as settlers. So, legally, at least so far as the settlement program was concerned, they were members of the Merhabete community. They were very distinct in appearance, however, much darker in complexion and with more rounded features, clearly of different ethnic origin. They were of generally lower social status, conflict averse and quiet living, not leaders in any sense, not fully incorporated into the life of the village, although not in any strict way excluded either. It was a line sensed more than defined.

The farmers I knew best generally viewed the end of slavery as a good thing. Several would speak with quiet disapproval of the ex-slave traders' past business. The former slave traders lived under a shadow, not a dark one, but it was something one knew about them and kept in mind. Still, there was no law against being an ex-slave trader and the live-and-let-live value of village life permitted them to be participants in village life. I don't recall them ever being asked to help resolve disputes, however, despite being of an age where one would expect them to play that role. Nevertheless, they were Merhabete. The ex-slaves really were not and were often the subjects of mild ridicule, mostly behind their backs.

The lone man still living as a slave died, locked in his master's house one night when the master had gone to Sodo and stayed over. The slave had been sick. The dynamics of this relationship were hard to fathom, impossible for me to understand. Everyone knew that slavery was illegal. The slave had ample, daily opportunities to escape. In fact, locking him in was more symbolic than restrictive since the walls of the house were, like mine, made of branches, easily cut through. The floor was the ground, easily dug through. I had asked people from time to time whether the master-slave relationship should be reported to the authorities, something I would not normally consider given the corruption certainly to be encountered in that quarter. The consistent response was to not stir things up, the same response from farmers, an ex-slave, and a schoolteacher.

"The police know about it anyway," I'd be told. "Everybody does."

"He is a slave, isn't he?" I'd ask, just to make sure I correctly understood this situation.

"Yes, that's right." And the respondent would tend to look away or at the ground, apparently made uncomfortable by the question.

Not seeing any action that I could usefully take, I let it go, always with doubts, mentally filing it in the category of cultural divides that I could never cross, or fathom.

THE DROUGHT

When, in 1973, it became clear that the rain was coming late, concern spread and then deepened. Those who earlier had expressed confidence that the rain would start soon eventually lapsed into the sullen silence of everyone else.

The river, which normally emptied into the lake maybe an hour's walk downstream, no longer flowed that far. The river soon shrank to little more than a trickle where it passed the village, then dried up altogether. To collect water people dug holes where the main channel normally flowed, very hard work in the rocky riverbed. Before long we had to go upstream from the village to get water, first just a short trek up the broad wide stretch, then around the bend where it narrowed and normally a rather deep pool sat below a large boulder. The pool was a reliable source for a week or so, then it was necessary to move further upstream.

The utter reliance we all had on a fresh water source had never been clearer to me. The village was located where it was *because* of the river. What would happen if the river dried up completely? What would people do? Where would they go? I imagined a sudden mass departure, but in what direction, with what objective? Would people leave all of their belongings behind? What of their animals?

The heat became so intense that it was uncomfortable to walk on paths. The ground was blistering. Where possible I took to walking on the brown, crinkly grass along the edge of paths because of the slight insulation from the sunbaked ground this provided.

About this time, we began to see refugees from the much drier northern provinces migrating south, desperately poor people with literally no place to go. Moving sometimes in small knots, other times in groups of several dozen at a time, they appeared resigned, discouraged, but still pressing on, seeking somewhere to land. The Emperor had barred drought refugees from entering the capital yet they were on the move, those who could, hundreds of thousands of them, seeking water, food, shelter, help.

Given the number of refugees on the move, there was little that anyone could do for those who passed through Wajifo. I would give something to drink, a little food to any individuals who stopped by my door. Many of the Merhabete and the Gemu did the same. But the problem far exceeded the village's ability to address in a way commensurate with the challenge. It was a challenge the government needed to be addressing but wasn't.

I knew a young economist, an American, working in one of the offices of the Agriculture Ministry who told me, on a visit to Addis Abeba, that he'd written a report predicting widespread famine due to the intense and spreading drought.

"What happened to the report?" I asked.

"It was immediately classified."

"But you've got to get it out," I said. "People have to know."

138

"I can't get it out. I don't have it anymore. I can't get to it. It's classified and I don't have access to classified documents."

"That's insane. You wrote it."

"I know," he laughed.

"But aren't you going to try to get the gist of your report out? You need to let people know about this. Maybe the UN, the FAO? Or the International Herald Tribune or someone?"

"The Ministry will know who did it."

"So what? I mean, who gives a damn about the Ministry of Agriculture?"

"They'll kick me out of the country."

He wouldn't budge. He felt he'd done his job and now it was up to the government of Ethiopia to take responsible action, not that he expected that to happen soon. Or at all.

He guessed that the government wanted to avoid panic, as if starving people would somehow be frightened by a bureaucrat's report predicting conditions they were already experiencing. My guess was that the government wanted no evidence that it had been forewarned. At any rate, the Emperor's forces succeeded in keeping the masses out of the capital. Hundreds of thousands died, mostly in the north, but largely out of sight so the Empire's dignity was preserved.

BAHYLU'S THEFT

I noticed one day that some money was missing from my desk drawer. I'd thought some money had gone missing earlier but I hadn't counted it beforehand and wasn't certain how much I'd had in the drawer. This time it was clear. Not wanting to believe it, I'd counted and recounted and knew for sure that 40 *birr* was missing now and I suspected the earlier apparent discrepancies were real. Money had gone missing in installments. I mentioned this to Brehane and to Haile, the student of a friend who was staying at my place for a few days. They immediately started to defend themselves against the possibility that I suspected them, and were visibly relieved when I assured them I had no such thing in mind. But still, a thief had somehow entered the house and taken money from a drawer just a few feet from my bed.

Since at least one of us had been at the house, or the house had been locked, all the time for the past few days, how did someone get in? Haile quickly found the answer, a small rip in the bamboo matting where it was nailed to the doorframe, just a few inches from the sliding bolt that secured the door. I went outside and stuck my hand through the opening. In a moment I was grasping the bolt, sliding it into the unlocked position. Then I simply opened the door and entered the house.

Both Haile and Brehane were certain that whoever was taking the money was operating on the theory that I would not notice if he took just a portion of the total each theft. They were also certain that with so many people around during the day, the thief was coming at night and would return. I thought their theory about the incremental nature of the thefts was probably accurate since it reflected my impression that money had gone missing without me being certain how much. The thief's tactic had worked.

I thought of just nailing the bamboo matting back to the doorframe but it seemed better to find out who was doing this and put a stop to it. So we decided not to tell anyone in the village, to avoid tipping off the thief, and instead to lie in wait for him that night.

There was a spot very near the door where it was possible to peer through the matting and see if anyone was at the door. We waited there for some time that night, keeping a quiet watch. But eventually the dark and the silence got to me and I began to doze off. I went to bed, asking that one of them wake me so I could take my turn when one or both of them had to sleep.

Maybe an hour or so later, Haile gently shook me awake and whispered in my ear, "The thief."

He pointed silently toward the door that was quietly being opened and closed from the outside, as if someone were trying to decide whether it was safe to enter. As I moved toward the door, our visitor seemed to sense that something wasn't right - a slight sound or maybe a tension in the air. The door banged shut and we heard footsteps running away into the darkness.

I started to follow but Haile grabbed my arm. "It was Bahylu," he said. "I saw him clearly. It was Bahylu and he had a club."

Brehane was also awake now and was shocked to hear his older brother's name. "Are you sure?" he asked.

"I'm certain. I watched him for a few minutes. It was Bahylu."

I was stunned. Not just because Bahylu was a close friend but because I'd recently taken him to the hospital in Sodo to repair his failing eyesight. So this revelation was a huge emotional blow. Still, it was important to remain calm and deal with the problem at hand.

"Well," I said, "he left heading toward the river, away from his house, so he'll need to make a circle to get home. Why don't one of you come with me and we can wait there until he shows up."

Walking rapidly through the silent village, Haile and I covered the three or four hundred meters to Kebede's place in a few moments. Kebede lived next-door to Bahylu. I called to Kebede in a low voice and when he came out I explained quickly what had happened. He gasped, slapping his hand to his face. We moved over to Bahylu's house and in a few moments Bahylu appeared out of the night, breathless. Seeing us, he tossed the club aside and sauntered over casually.

"Pee," he managed. "I had to pee."

He was catching his breath. We all stood there in uncomfortable silence for a few moments until it occurred to Bahylu to ask what the three of us were doing there.

"You know why we're here," Kebede answered sternly. "You didn't have to run to pee. Give Bill back his money, all of it, right now."

"What money?"

"All of it. This is your chance."

"I don't understand," Bahylu muttered. "I'm going back to bed."

"Don't be crazy. Don't be a thief."

"Good night," Bahylu responded and went inside.

Kebede turned to me and grasped my hand. "We can solve this in the morning, Bill. We can solve this," he said earnestly. "We have a way. Please don't go to the police first."

The police were in Mirab Abaye, maybe half an hour distant by bus, but I had no intention of going there.

144

"I'm not going to the police," I said, "but I want my money back."

"Good. I'll come over to your house early in the morning."

Walking back to my house, Haile challenged me. "You should have told someone else, one of the elders. They're brothers – Kebede and Bahylu. Brehane too. You can't trust them to be honest about this. I like Brehane but now that we know it was Bahylu you shouldn't trust Brehane either.

"I know. But I trust them. Kebede and Brehane didn't know about this, I'm sure. I think Kebede will do the right thing. He's honest. We've helped each other before."

Back at the house, Brehane searched my face for a hint of suspicion. "Should I leave?" he asked me. "Do you want me to leave? I'll go tonight if you think I had anything to do with this."

"No, of course not. He's your brother. He's not you. I know you're honest. I trust Kebede too. We'll take care of this tomorrow."

"If you go to the police they'll arrest me too. Since I live here they'll think I told Bahylu about the money."

"I know, but I'm not going to the police. They'll want bribes and they don't know any more about this than we do anyway. We can solve it here. Believe me, I trust you. Now let's all get some sleep."

"You're sure?"

"Yes. I'm completely sure."

Haile was watching this exchange with intense interest. He seemed on the verge of speaking several times but caught himself. Finally, he caught my eye, gestured hopelessly but said nothing and eventually went to bed.

The next morning Kebede appeared at my door early and laid out his plan. He asked me who had been in my house the last several days. I named everyone I could think of and it was a small group, maybe six or seven farmers, including Bahylu. Kebede sent someone to ask them to gather in my house and explained to me that while all of them stayed in my house, he and two other farmers would search their houses one by one of to see if the money could be found. By keeping them all together no one would be able to go back home and hide the money somewhere else. I reminded him that we had virtually caught Bahylu in the act of breaking in and asked why we didn't just go to his house.

Kebede explained that he was also sure it was Bahylu but this way everyone would be treated equally, the money would be found in daylight by three people at once rather than relying on the word of Haile, whom nobody really knew. Telling people that Haile saw Bahylu breaking in would not go over well in the village; people might think Haile himself stole the money and framed Bahylu.

"This is how we do it," Kebede concluded.

I knew he was right. Still, while it was the Merhabete custom to handle issues internally, and though this was the specific approach for dealing with theft, it was uncommon for a family member to be the intermediary. But I trusted Kebede implicitly so I agreed.

The farmers who gathered at my house later also assured me that this was how it was done, although these assurances were given in ignorance of Bahylu's guilt. Kebede, Bogali, and someone else went out to search the houses after reminding us all that no one should be allowed to leave the house until they came back.

We all made the best of it, although Bahylu's feigned ease was not convincing. I put on some tea. After fifteen minutes or so Bahylu announced that he had to pee and stepped out the back of the house. When he didn't come back in, someone looked out back and it was clear he was gone.

The group was very upset, knowing instinctively that Bahylu was the thief and fearing that he'd collect the money in his house and hide it in one of theirs. I asked everyone else to stay there while I went to alert Kebede and the others but as I stepped out the door the three house searchers came up the path. They had the money — one hundred *birr* - that they'd found in Bahylu's house. They'd encountered Bahylu, running to his house, just as they'd emerged with the money in hand.

Kebede was both livid and embarrassed. Yet Bahylu was still his brother. He asked me to meet with Bahylu, to let him talk with me and, of course, I agreed. We walked over to Bahylu's house. Kebede called to him and Bahylu came out slowly, looking at the ground.

"This is your chance, you thief," Kebede barked. "Talk to Bill. Now. Thank God he hasn't gone to the police. Talk!"

Bahylu took me by the hand and began walking in a large circle. He begged my forgiveness, promised to give me back all that he had stolen, which he admitted was almost three hundred birr in total but he had spent more than half of it. That explained why only one hundred birr was discovered in his house.

He said that he himself could barely believe what he'd done. It was like he'd gone crazy. I was his close friend and had helped him so many times. I had given him his eyesight back when I took him to the hospital that time. We'd had such good times together. I had taken in his brother, was helping him get through school. And so forth.

"Please don't go to the police," he finished.

I had no intention of going to the police. I was committed to solving this problem in the village, in the family. The police were outsiders and, it was always safe to assume, corrupt and potentially violent. So, no, I was not going there. I assured Bahylu of that but told him that the money he'd stolen was intended for projects in the village and I needed it back. He finally looked at me, though barely making eye contact, hugged me and thanked me. We sat down with Kebede and worked out a repayment plan.

It was never the same again with Bahylu. His reputation in the village had gone sour. And even though he did, with Kebede's prompting, pay back most of the money more or less on schedule, our easy relationship was gone. How could it be otherwise?

Two or three months later Bahylu took sick again, a respiratory problem, and traveled to the mission hospital in Sodo by himself. Kebede was up in Merhabete country at the time and Brehane had distanced himself from Bahylu since the theft and wasn't keeping track of him. He'd been gone for about a week before his young wife told her father, Bogali, that she was concerned. A day or two later Bogali took the bus to Sodo and went by the hospital. It turned out that Bahylu had been very sick and had died within a day or so of his arrival there. Bogali said it had been a very painful death. I didn't want to know the details. The hospital staff hadn't known where Bahylu came from or whom to contact so they simply buried him in a place maintained for burying unclaimed bodies. He'd been buried for a few days by the time we all learned of his death.

I heard from several people that this is how God works. This was justice. I had helped Bahylu when he needed help. I had given him back his eyesight and he had used his vision to steal from me. So God saw to it that he died alone, with fever and pain, without family or friends present, and was buried by strangers without ceremony or mourning.

This seemed a bit severe for stealing a few dollars, even for God. But no one's ever called Him lighthearted, I guess. It was sad to see Bahylu go so unlamented. Brehane, of course, mourned him. And I felt deprived of the chance to reach some new level of understanding and maybe trust with Bahylu. We had been friends and it was sad to think of him dying alone, among strangers.

KEBEDE SEEKS A CURE

Kebede had been having nosebleeds, fairly severe ones, but they didn't seem to be interfering with his life or work. He asked me if I had any medicine or knew of any way to treat nosebleeds, or control them. I didn't, so I suggested that he might want to try the hospital in Sodo, to see what they could do. But Kebede was a traditionalist. He probably would have taken medicine from me because we knew each other well and I'd taken care of minor injuries and ailments in the past, but he was inclined toward traditional cures. Once, despite my protests, he'd cut long slits into his young sons' cheeks when they had the mumps. When the mumps eventually went away, he was convinced his treatment had worked. That was his style, so he wasn't about to go into the foreign world of a mission hospital.

One evening his two little sons appeared at the door asking me to go over to Kebede's house. He was really sick, they said, so I followed them over and found him passed out on his bed with blood pouring from his nose. Someone was catching it in a small pot as it came down the side of his face.

"What can we do?" his wife asked me.

This was well beyond anything I felt competent to address. I touched his forehead and his arm. The skin felt cool and clammy. I had no suggestions beyond getting him to the hospital, but it was late and that was clearly out of the question for the night. The house was full. It felt like a death vigil and for good reason. I sat on the edge of the bed, squeezed in with several friends and family members, trying

151

to conjure up a helpful idea. None came and eventually the close quarters felt oppressive. I thought we should all pull back a little and give Kebede some space to breathe, but I knew enough not to suggest that so I left, beginning to feel resigned to Kebede's death by morning. Brehane followed after a while, looking downcast. I made some tea and we sat across from each other sipping our tea and not saying much.

But Kebede didn't die. The bleeding eventually stopped and sometime in the morning his eyes flickered open. When I stopped by, he was propped up, looking pale and weak but alive. The pot of blood was still there, saved for some reason. Flies buzzed around it in the heat.

"I'm like an ox," he smiled. "Look at all the blood I lost and I'm still alive.

"People asked me if I saw God when I was asleep," he went on, "but I saw nothing. Heard nothing. It was like I was dead but I didn't see God. Nothing happened. Just silence. It was black and silent."

"Well, maybe now it would be a good idea to go to the hospital," I suggested. "I'll go up there with you if you'd like. I can talk to the people there for you. We can catch a bus today. This morning."

He shook his head. "No, I'm better now. But I do need to be treated so I'm going back up to Merhabete country as soon as I can get back on my feet. There are some good

healers up there. They can heal anything. I'm going to go in
a day or two."

"I'm sure they're good," I lied, "but it's a long way. The
hospital is a lot closer. Why don't we try the hospital first?
Then, when you've rested and are a little better, then go up
to Merhabete and see the healer. What do you think?"

"I'll try Merhabete medicine first and if that doesn't work I'll
go to the hospital."

I knew when an argument with Kebede was settled and this
one was settled so we talked about other things until he
dozed off.

Kebede sold some grain and took off three days later. I'd
bought him some meat on market day. His wife prepared it
and we passed a pleasant evening together the night before
his departure.

A couple of weeks later, word came from Kebede to
Brehane. Kebede needed money. The treatments were not
going well and he'd decided to go to a hospital. He asked
that his wife sell some corn and give the money to Brehane
who would then travel to Merhabete as quickly as possible.
The nosebleeds had continued. Kebede was very sick.

Arrangements were quickly made. I gave Brehane money for
transport and food. I called a friend in Addis Abeba from
the phone center in Sodo and asked him to meet Brehane at

the Addis Abeba bus station, give him a place for the night and get him on the right bus, for the north, the next day. He was only about fourteen and had never undertaken a trip of any length by himself before. When these arrangements were in place he was off.

Two weeks later, Brehane was back looking worn and distressed. The day before he'd arrived to deliver the money to Kebede the healer had built a smoky fire. Then, with the help of Kebede's parents and two brothers who lived in Merhabete, the healer pinned Kebede to the ground next to the fire and covered him and the fire with cow hides and blankets to trap the smoke.

The idea was to dry out his nasal passages and lungs so that the bleeding would stop. Instead, he suffocated and died. Someone had told Brehane that Kebede died struggling to get up, pleading with those sitting on him, pinning him to the ground, to free him, to wait for his brother Brehane to arrive.

"If you had come sooner, he'd still be alive."

MENGISTU'S LAND

Along with the other initial group of Merhabete settlers, Mengistu had been granted ten hectares of land in Wajifo by the Emperor.

These land grants were the basis for the Wajifo settlement. Little of the land had been farmed before, at least not in recent history. Some may have been taken from the local Gemu who had used it from time to time, but for the most part it was forest, needing to be cleared before it could be tilled. Since the land grants had come from the Emperor and since the Merhabete were Amhara, the politically dominant ethnic group, ownership seemed quite secure and the Merhabete proceeded with land clearance, confident that they were developing their own land.

The grants were part of an effort to resettle landless or land-poor peasants from the crowded northern highlands into the relatively sparsely settled south. And within the southern province of Gemu Gofa, special attention was directed to Wajifo where the soil was deep, heavy, and black. The land grants stretched broadly for several kilometers along the floor of the Rift Valley.

The Merhabete were proud of their status as landowners, proud to be farmers, and proud of their work in clearing the land and establishing their farms. The Merhabete tended to look down on the Gemu as a group but over time friendships were formed between individuals.

The Gemu were generally less assertive, more accepting culturally, and seemed to regard the Merhabete presence as a fact of life. So, despite some early resentment on the part of the Gemu, relations between the two groups were remarkably benign, if not initially friendly. The occasional confrontation was more often linked, at least immediately, to some individual transgression, maybe a drunken fight on market day, than to any mass ethnic hostility.

After I'd been in Wajifo about a year, Mengistu received a summons to appear in court in Chencha, up in the highlands over the western rim of the valley and south of Wajifo. The summons had to do with his land title and, though a bit concerned about it, his initial outward reaction was one of mildly amused indignation. Didn't they know who he was? Mengistu had a title.

Opinion was split among the other farmers. Some, especially the younger ones, felt he had nothing to worry about. Everyone knew that Hailie Selassie himself had granted the Merhabete this land. Besides, things had been going well for Mengistu. He had cleared two or three hectares, his harvests so far had been good, he was learning to read, had a child on the way. He was almost always in a positive frame of mind, full of wit and humor.

The older farmers were more cautious in their assessment. Anything that involved the court system was not good news. They knew from experience that the rich and the connected had the advantage.

Regardless, Mengistu had to go to court so the next day he was off to Chencha, maybe a twelve-hour walk up out of the Valley and south along the edge of the highlands. He returned late the following day. It had just been an initial hearing, a brief explanation of the case. Neguse, a large land-owner whose holdings abutted Mengistu's land, was contesting Mengistu's title. His representative claimed that Neguse was the rightful owner of the land, that Mengistu stole it, and must return the land and pay rent for the time he farmed it. The court would be in touch.

When the Merhabete had first settled in Wajifo there had been no real road to the village, just a dirt track. But the subsequent construction of the road, though still a gravel and dirt road with no bridges, had opened up the entire area all the way to Arba Minch, the provincial capital, about two hours south.

Four-wheel-drive buses began traveling occasionally, then regularly from Sodo to Arba Minch with stops in Wajifo, and all the other settlements and villages along the route. Competition was fierce among the handful of bus companies seeking to dominate the trade. Tires were slashed, drivers or their assistants were beaten, occasionally shots were fired, buses would swerve dangerously as their drivers tried to literally force the competition off the road. Seyoum, a wealthy businessman, emerged victorious, at least for a while on the Sodo–Arba Minch route. He began looking around for new opportunities. With the road providing new access to urban markets, investment in agriculture looked promising. He decided to focus on land.

Despite the fact that the threat came from Neguse rather than Seyoum, Mengistu's land "dispute" was, in effect, a test case to see just how secure these Emperor-granted titles really were. So, with no legitimate claim on the land, and despite the fact that Mengistu's title document had described his land as having been government land, Neguse had gone to court to claim Mengistu's land as his own.

Months went by and the court summonses began arriving with greater frequency, cutting into time that Mengistu needed to spend managing his fields. It also became a financial drain. With sufficient notice he had time to take the Sodo bus south to Arba Mich, then switch to one of the small, tough, four-wheel-drive buses that made the climb up the twisting, rocky road to Chencha and the court. Early morning court appointments required him to travel the day before and pay for a place to stay. All of this cost money that he really didn't have. Not much actually happened in court, of course, but he didn't dare ignore a summons. They were trying to wear down his resistance.

The judge began asking for bribes to keep the case going. When Mengistu initially declined to pay, the judge, speaking from the bench, reminded him that, "Justice is expensive," and threatened repercussions unless Mengistu began paying his share. I began giving him small amounts of money to help cover his expenses then, hating to do it, a bit more money to cover the miserable little bribes the judge demanded. Meanwhile, the judge and Neguse, old friends, regularly could be seen drinking together in Neguse's bar.

Early one evening, a friend of Mengistu's appeared at his house panting and sweating, clearly exhausted. He had hurried all the way from Chencha with urgent news. The judge had set an appointment for the following morning without the usual notification. The judge was spreading the word that if Mengistu were to miss the court session he would find in favor of Neguse. Everyone, Mengistu's friend told him, expected him to miss the appointment. Neguse's friends and supporters - and those who now hoped to be counted among that select group once the great man had won his case – were already celebrating in Chencha.

This was desperately bad news. The morning bus, with its connection in Arba Minch, would take too long. It was too late to set out by foot for Chencha. Hiking for hours up out of the Valley in the darkness, through forests and grassland inhabited by lions, hyenas and poisonous snakes, then down the upland dirt road into town late at night with the risk of being robbed, was simply out of the question. But making the same trip in the morning would get him into Chencha only in time to learn that he'd lost the case and make him the object of ridicule by Neguse's supporters and courthouse hangers on.

By a stroke of luck, my friend Bernard was visiting. In fact, we were having supper with Mengistu and Bekelech whenMengistu's friend arrived. While his friend washed his hands, accepted some *tela* and joined us all around the dinner tray, Bernard and I conferred about what could be done. I had commitments in the village the next day, but since Bernard had his jeep and a pretty open schedule, the solution was obvious; he and Mengistu would depart for Chencha before sunrise.

The rest of the evening was spent vying with each other to express the greatest contempt for Neguse and for the corrupt system that empowered him. Word of this latest outrage had spread around the village and soon we had plenty of help condemning the bad guys, lamenting the plight of poor farmers, and, of course, finishing the *tela*.

Bernard, Mengistu, and his friend departed on schedule in the early morning darkness. Mengistu's friend got out of the jeep a few kilometers before Chencha to avoid being identified publicly in town as the undercover agent of justice, and Bernard and Mengistu arrived in Chencha just in time for the court appointment. While Bernard went looking for coffee, Mengistu walked over to the courthouse. His presence there was utterly unexpected, so much so that at first it went unnoticed.

The case was announced from the bench. Then the presence of the parties was ascertained.

"Is Neguse present?"

"I am here representing Neguse," his advocate responded.

"Mengistu Gilmariam? Is he here?"

Several people, responding at once, talking over each other, garbled the message that he was not present.

So again, from the bench: "Mengistu Gilmariam?"

"He is not present," one voice responded, immediately and clearly this time.

A smile began to spread across the judge's face, and the advocate spread his hands in a gesture that asked, are we finished now?

Then Mengistu, from the back of the court-room, spoke into the silence.

"He's not here? Then who am I?"

This wasn't in the script. A hubbub ensued as the audience, who'd thought it knew the plot, craned its collective neck to get a look at this impudent farmer while the judge demanded silence and order in the court.

"Who are you then?" the judge scowled, squinting nearsightedly toward the back.

"I'm Mengistu Gilmariam."

Again, turmoil in the court. Mengistu had ruined everything. He sensed general frustration in the audience and clear anger from the judge. Mengistu's bribes had been utterly inadequate and the judge would have liked nothing more than to earn the enduring friendship of wealthy Neguse by finding quickly in his favor. But this tenacious farmer simply could not be shaken loose. The fact that Mengistu was Amhara was probably not helpful to the judge, and the land title having been bestowed by the Emperor was at least an irksome, if not major inconvenience.

Perhaps his pique caused the judge to momentarily lose his footing. He knew the basis for Mengistu's claim and yet muttered something about bringing this case to resolution once and for all. Then, unadvisedly, he demanded, "You keep saying this is your land, that it was granted to you but I don't believe it! Who gave it to you?"

Mengistu again waited for quiet.

Then, his voice loud and clear, "His Highness Hailie Selassie granted it to me. And, if there is justice, only His Highness can take it away."

Stunned silence. No Gemu Gofa judge was going to challenge that assertion. However annoyed the judge may have been, he was not about to go on record siding with a locally prominent land-owner against His Imperial Majesty – King of Kings, Elect of God, and Conquering Lion of the Tribe of Judah.

After a quick, animated conversation with Neguse's advocate the judge announced that this case would have to be continued, date to be announced. He had other cases to try.

162

Outside the court-house a small crowd gathered around Mengistu, surprising him with expressions of support and best wishes. The townspeople patted him on the back and grabbed his hand, clearly delighted to see the judge flummoxed and, at least for the moment, the wealthy Neguse frustrated by an ordinary guy. I'm sure they also loved the theatrical dimension of Mengistu's arrival and his performance in court. He was escorted to a nearby *tej bet,* a *tej* bar, to celebrate before locating Bernard and heading back to Wajifo.

Surrounded by friends in Wajifo, Mengistu took great pleasure in recounting his court adventure. Unfortunately, this was a short-lived psychological victory for Mengistu. Neguse was a frustrated, wealthy man. And frustrated, wealthy men whose court cases did not go as planned would not enhance the judge's own financial status. This case, this test case, had presented the judge with a potentially steady income stream and, if it turned out well, Neguse saw a partner in challenging the other Wajifo farmers' land claims.

The summonses became still more frequent, increasing the time Mengistu needed to spend defending his land tenure and reducing his confidence that he'd ultimately prevail. The travel costs and bribes began to add up as well.

Life was also becoming difficult on the home front for Mengistu. He and his wife, Bekelech, began fighting. Their baby was born. And then died four months later.

One evening he stayed later than the rest of a group of farmers who had stopped by my house for tea. He fidgeted with some small objects on my table. I offered more tea but he declined. Then, not seeming to know what else to do, he said he would have some more tea but didn't touch it after I'd filled his cup.

"What is it?" I asked. "What's the matter?"

"I'm fine."

"No, you're not. Did something happen?"

"No. I should go." But he made no effort to stand up.

"Is it Neguse?"

"Yes. No. It's something. About Neguse. About Chencha, what happened in Chencha. On my last trip to court."

"What happened?"

He sighed deeply, leaning over, staring intently at the table. His hands clasped tightly on his knees.

"I hate Neguse. I hate this government. My whole life is worthless."

"The case isn't over yet, is it? You didn't lose, did you?"

His face dropped closer to the table. It was almost on the table. I was staring at the top of his head.

"I spent some of the money you gave me on a prostitute in Chencha. Now I have a disease. And I didn't give the judge as much as he wanted."

"So he wants more."

"Yes. And Bekelech is very angry."

"I wish you hadn't done that. There's a limit on how much money I can give you. And I don't give it to you for prostitutes."

"I know. I was drinking *tej*. It just happened."

"What does Bekelech want?"

"She wants me to move out. I'm sleeping at Tesfaye's house for now."

"That's pretty crowded, isn't it? Do you want to stay here?"

"This is too far from our house. She won't know where I am and she'll think I'm with another woman. We can hear each other from Tesfaye's. She can check on me."

His head was up now. Things were in the open.

"She can check on you."

"Yes."

We stared at each other across the table. Mengistu offered a rueful smile and shrugged. I returned the gesture.

"Now what?" I asked. "What do you want? What do we do?"

"I was hoping you could help me get rid of this," he said, pointing at his genitals.

"Get rid of that? Are you sure?"

"I mean the disease," he smiled.

"Well, I've been thinking we should maybe go to the Ministry of Land Reform in Addis Abeba to see if anyone there could be helpful on the case with Neguse. There must be something they can do. You have a title to your land."

166

"But what about . . ."

"And then we could check with a doctor up there. I may be able to get you in to see the Peace Corps doctor. That way maybe we won't have to pay."

"When?"

"I don't know. The day after tomorrow? We can stay at Bernard's place in Addis Abeba."

"OK. Bekelech will think I'm going to see prostitutes in Addis Abeba."

"Should I talk with her?"

"Yes. First me, then you. She'll believe you."

Mengistu shared the plan with Bekelech that night or early the next morning because she was at my door to confirm his story when I was having coffee just after sunrise.

She was angry and suspicious of him, understandably. She tried to engage me on the medical issue. I tried to stay absolutely neutral on that subject, just confirming the dual purpose of our trip to Addis Abeba and concentrating on the land title objective. But she kept pushing the issue and I found myself expressing some understanding of Mengistu's predicament. He's been under a lot of pressure, he was drinking, if it weren't for Neguse and the court case none of this would be happening.

"I just want all this to be over," I told her, "so the three of us can enjoy a nice meal together again, that's what I want. I miss you two. Things are really hard right now."

Bekelelch sighed. "I think the same thing. But Mengistu is changing" she said. "He's angry a lot. But you're right that the land problem is the cause of all this."

"Neguse is going to win this," she said emphatically. "The rich people always win."

"Well, I agree that's usually true. Almost always true, but let's see what we can do in Addis Abeba."

We talked about other things, found something to laugh about. She said she trusted me and understood what I'd said about Mengistu. Things would be better between them later on she hoped. But she still planned to keep him out of the house for a while longer.

"I'll make him suffer for a while," she smiled.

"I understand that. He does too, I think."

"Have a good trip. And thank you for your help."

I was glad to get through that conversation without causing a rift with Bekelech. I was still annoyed with Mengistu but couldn't help but feel sympathetic to him, as well.

The trip to Addis Abeba solved Mengistu's medical embarrassment easily enough.

The land tenure issue was another story.

Walking into the Ministry of Land Reform, we made a couple of inquiries and soon found ourselves meeting with two young, enthusiastic lawyers. They were very sympathetic and certain that this problem could be solved in Mengistu's favor. He was so clearly in the right.

They were excited to meet a poor farmer confronting the kind of corruption and exploitation that they and their Ministry were there to confront and alleviate. This was not an abstract point of law. This was the real thing and they were going to see justice done. The meeting ended with hearty handshakes and good feelings all around. We were to come back the next morning after they'd researched the case further, prepared some paper-work and cleared things with their supervisors.

We left giddy with excitement.

"I knew this would be worthwhile," I said, naively.

But Mengistu was already calming down, realizing that nothing had really changed. Neguse still wanted his land. The judge still wanted his bribes. We'd just met with some decent, well-intentioned guys who clearly wanted to help, intended to help, but Mengistu was wisely reining in his expectations.

I tried to follow his lead but there was something about being in the capital city. Maybe it was the clear, cool air at this high elevation, the bustling streets, or the fact that we'd just met with lawyers at the Ministry that made me feel that this dispute in one of the outlying provinces would be seen for what it was, a tawdry land grab, and it would now be resolved quickly and justly. We had come to the right place.

My optimism was short-lived. By the next morning everything returned to normal. The young lawyers were embarrassed and rather sheepish. It turned out that the case was more complicated than they'd thought. Their boss, or someone higher up, had made some calls to Gemu Gofa. Someone had spoken with Neguse. The provincial governor had been contacted. There was nothing the Ministry could do to be helpful. They were very sorry.

"Is there someone else we can talk with?" I asked. "Someone you think could be helpful?"

They looked at each other. "Well, our boss wanted to talk with you when you came back today," one of them volunteered.

"OK, that sounds good."

One of them went to set up the meeting. While he was gone the other one came around his desk, pulled us close, and in a hushed voice advised us that we were not going to like what his boss had to say but, whatever we felt, we should not argue with him.

"He's powerful. He can cause trouble for you." Then, looking at me, "Maybe you don't know our country very well . . ." He glanced at Mengistu, seeming to assess how much trust he should invest in this peasant farmer.

"I know a bit about the country. I've lived here for a while . ." I started to say.

"There's corruption. Almost everywhere," he whispered.

Mengistu and I both smiled, in spite of ourselves.

"I know," we said simultaneously.

"You know. So you know there's really nothing my colleague and I can do to help you." He searched our faces.

"It's not your fault," Mengistu assured him quietly, and I was suddenly embarrassed for this intelligent, committed lawyer whom any well-meaning organization would be proud to have on staff.

The door to the next office opened and in moments we were in the presence of a well-dressed yet somehow scruffy looking middle-aged man with a tired face but impatient manner.

Our audience was short. He'd looked into Mengistu's claim, he informed us, and found it to be without merit. He'd spoken with the most senior officials in Gemu Gofa and they had assured him that Neguse had a strong case and that, anyway, the case was in the courts and that's where it should be resolved. The Ministry had decided not to get involved.

Mengistu started to ask a question. "That's all I have to say on that," our host cut him off.

"Now, what's your role in this case?" he asked me, not challenging really, but with more than curiosity in his voice.

"I have no role. I'm just a friend of Mengistu. I came to Addis Abeba with him and helped him find the Ministry. That's all. I work in the community development program in the village but I'm not really formally involved in the case."

"Good. As a foreigner you should stay out of it." This didn't sound like an order, more like serious advice intended to end the conversation. I took it to be the last word. Until he added flatly, "It could be dangerous."

"Thank you."

"Anything else? No? Good. Someone will show you out."

We were escorted out and one of the young lawyers accompanied us out of the building. He seemed to be trying to organize his thoughts. Finally, he took our hands, and confided quietly, "There are powerful people down there, where you're from. They have money and connections. People are afraid." He paused. "My boss is not a bad man," he added and with that he headed back into the building.

With no alternative strategy to the one that had just failed we caught the bus back to Wajifo.

It was almost too late in the season to plant but Mengistu started preparing the ground anyway and got a little cotton planted when another summons from Chencha arrived. He headed back to the court but without hope and decided that he would not finish planting since his crop, however pitiful, would likely go to Neguse when he won the case, as Mengistu was now certain would be the outcome.

And he was right. The court ruled against him. He lost his land, had to pay court expenses, plus three years back rent to Neguse.

Mengistu began seeking day labor work among the other farmers and whatever other jobs he could pick up in the marketplace – unloading trucks at Mohammed's and the like. He was in a near-permanent state of domestic warfare with Bekelech, finding fault with everything she did, including the quality of the *tela* she made to sell by the drink on market day. Our meals together, with their easy-going hospitality, wide ranging conversations, and simple but really delicious food became a thing of the past. I seldom saw him anymore.

Then one day, while Mengistu was engaged in field work for another farmer, Bekelech appeared at my door. She had decided to leave Mengistu, she told me, and needed my help to do it without creating a scene or inciting violence.

"Has he hit you?" I asked. One of the things I always liked about Mengistu was that, like Tamtim, he didn't hit his wife. Tamtim didn't because he was obviously and completely in love; Mengistu because he thought it was bad behavior. Also, I think, he was a little afraid of Bekelech. She was a strong woman.

"No, he has never hit me. But he might if he knew I was leaving. I don't think he would just watch me walk away and get on the bus."

"What can I do?"

"I'd like to bring my belongings, the things I'm taking with me, here to your house, today, and leave them here. Then, just before the bus comes tomorrow, I'll pretend I'm going to the river for water, I'll leave the house with my water jug, and instead will stop here, pick up my things and catch the bus at the river."

"OK," I said. "That would be alright but this makes me sad. Mengistu is, or was, a good friend. I'd still help him out if I knew what to do but I understand why you're leaving." I paused. "One thing, Bekelech. Just please be sure that no one knows you're doing this with my help. I don't want to have to explain myself to, well, to anyone. I'll put your things in my room so even Brehane won't know about this."

"Don't worry," she assured me. "No one else will know."

So that's what we did. She came by in the morning. I gave her a little money for the road. She collected her things, kissed me on both cheeks, thanked me.

"Good bye, my brother."

"Goodbye, my sister."

And she was gone. A few minutes later I could hear the bus, radio blaring, heading toward the river. She did violate our little pact by bringing along a friend whose job was to take Bekelech's water jug and abandon it near the river. Otherwise it would be found at my place and conclusions drawn. Her friend, Almaz, and I looked at each other, made eye contact, but didn't exchange a word on the subject at hand. Not then, not ever.

Over the months that Mengistu's case had been unfolding, Seyoum, the bus company owner, was mimicking Mengistu's judicial experience by challenging the titles of other Merhabete farmers. Two additional large landowners took it even further and simply bulldozed the fields of targeted Gemu farmers, burned their huts and took the land. A common practice was to pay the Gemus about $30 when their land was taken. The Merhabete got nothing as it became obvious that their deeds were practically worthless.

As my fourth year was drawing to an end, only a third of the original settlers were still in Wajifo, and a third of them had lost their land in court cases. Others were still engaged in court actions. The corruption behind these figures is easily imagined and the tenacity, even bravery, of those who continued the fight for justice was awe inspiring, quite moving, and almost certainly hopeless.

TRADITIONAL CURES

People would call on me for help or advice on simple medical issues and I tried to be responsive. But they had their own treatments, as well, such as when Kebede cut long slits in his sons' cheeks to cure them of the mumps. And, in his eyes, it worked, the scars being a small price or side effect.

The Merhabete also had a cure for rabies. While I can't remember (probably never knew) all the steps, the general idea was that if someone was bitten by a bat the bat, or at least *a* bat, was caught, killed, and dried in the sun. It was then ground into powder, made into a tea, and the victim made to drink it. If the bat was rabid, the patient would throw up tiny bats and the disease would be cured. If they did not, either the bat was not rabid or the treatment hadn't worked. Reading the treatment results required some interpretative talent, I suppose. The same treatment was applied to dog bites although how the dog was dried in the sun I don't know. I never saw that treatment in practice.

One day Almaz and her husband, Bekele, came by with their baby, seeking help. The baby was suffering from constipation. To my surprise, in addition to breast feeding, they were using baby formula, which I had not seen in Wajifo. I'm not sure why and I was concerned that they were mixing powdered formula with what was reliably polluted water. But they didn't want to discuss that. They wanted to know if I had any ideas for curing the constipation. Speaking from personal experience, I suggested coffee.

"Don't give the baby much, she's so small, but a little bit in her formula might help," I suggested.

They were at my door early the next morning to happily report that my coffee remedy worked. I was almost as relieved as they were.

One evening as I was chatting with Habtu there was a knock on the door. I opened it to find a young Gemu boy who Habtu recognized from day school. He had been a student for a year or so and had then dropped out, presumably to help with farm work. I gestured for him to come in and he did and then, without saying anything, lifted his shirt to reveal several open, oozing sores on his chest and stomach. In obvious pain, he told Habtu in barely a whisper that his father had sent him over hoping I could provide a cure.

Trying to avoid inflicting much more pain than the boy was already experiencing, I gently cleaned his sores with antiseptic soap, smeared them with antibiotic ointment and asked him to return the next day.

He did. But his father had decided to complement my treatment with one of his own. He had filled the sores with cobwebs saturated with fine ash. He was careful to tuck the cobwebs under the skin around the edges of the sores.

I liked to think that over the years I had been patient and respectful, if quietly skeptical, of traditional treatments and cures. But this time I was angry. Maybe because the father had set back the healing process and now I had to undo his work, inflicting more excruciating pain on the boy, something we both found stressful. But the main reason, I think, was because I would be leaving Wajifo before long and was beginning to let my honest reactions prevail over my efforts to respect local custom. I was sick of pointless pain, and of pretending I didn't see it. I was also tired of injustice, cruelty, and exploitation. And there was too much of all of these in the village, in the country really.

"Stupid!" I said. "This is stupid. This is so stupid. Why would anyone do this?" I asked rhetorically. "Does this guy *want* to hurt his kid?"

Habtu, who had come back this second day to check on the boy, calmed me down. "They don't know," he said quietly. "They do things like this because they don't know any better."

"I know. I know why they do these things. They don't understand modern treatments and yet they feel they have to do something. But if he wants me to treat his son, then let me treat his son. This is, I don't know. This is cruel."

But, of course, Habtu was right to remain calm. I knew that and didn't want to scare the boy away so I set about clearing his sores of the dirty cobwebs. He shivered with pain. We were both sweating heavily by the time I finished and tears were running down his face.

I applied the antibiotic again and asked the boy if he wanted me to walk him back to his house. It was dark. But he had a flashlight and it wasn't very far, he said, so he'd be fine.

"Then look, tell your father I think that we should only try one treatment at a time. Two at a time doesn't work very well. And, if he agrees, come back tomorrow. We'll try my treatment first and if it doesn't work he can try his treatment."

Habtu reiterated my instructions and request. The boy thanked me, wished us a good night, and left. I never saw him again.

DOUBLE THREAT

Since my first night in Wajifo when my neighbor was killed, I was always vigilant about snakes, especially in my house. The walls, which were bundles of branches haphazardly covered with bamboo matting, had plenty of gaps large enough to accommodate just about any snake. I always slept with a flashlight and flicked it on to check whenever I thought I heard something unusual in the house.

One night, about six weeks before I was to leave Wajifo, I shuffled back inside from a late night pee. I crawled into bed, switched off the flashlight and had just started to drift back to sleep when I thought I heard a rustling in some dry leaves on the floor where the foot of the bed met the wall. Sleep was beckoning but I decided, groggily, that I'd better check this out.

Without getting up, I shined the light toward the dirt floor and thought I saw the tail end of a snake slithering through the dry leaves. Still not certain, but more awake, I leaned over the edge of the bed and trained the light along the ground. There was nothing. Sitting up, I shined it back down the length of my body, toward my feet. There, poking around the blanket was the head – and a foot or two more – of a good sized snake.

I froze for a moment.

Then, "Holy shit!"

I leapt out of bed. In my mind, I leapt as if in a cartoon – straight up while still horizontal, flipped around in mid-air, and landed on my feet next to the bed. That didn't happen, of course, but I was on my feet instantly and a second later was in the main room where Brehane was sleeping on a cot since he had just sprayed his room with insecticide that afternoon and the smell there was still quite strong.

"Brehane. Snake!" I yelled. "Snake. Snake. Get up!"

Instantly, Brehane went from deep sleep to standing on the cot. He stood there dizzy, rubbing his eyes, mumbling, "What? Where?"

"In my bed. In there," I pointed.

"Your bed? A snake?"

"Yes. A snake. In my bed. Or maybe on the ground now. It was trying to get into my bed."

"Can you see it?"

"Not from here."

"What'll we do? Kill it?"

"What else? I can't sleep with it. And I don't think you can sleep here with a snake right over there, can you?"

"No, I can't. Wait a minute. I'm not awake."

"Yes, you are."

Brehane ground his fists into his eyes, then slapped his hands against his face a few times.

"OK, I'm awake now. Let's do it."

We grabbed a spear and a shovel. I had the flashlight but it was beginning to go off and on, its light growing weaker.

"Where's your flashlight?" I asked.

"The batteries are dead."

We crept into my room and, to avoid stepping on the snake, I pointed the increasingly unreliable flashlight under the bed and around the floor generally. Nothing. The flashlight went dead. I shook it.

"Turn it on."

"I can't. Wait." I shook it again and it came on, briefly. Then darkness.

Since we couldn't see the snake we decided that it might be under the blanket, and on the count of three began to beat the blanket frantically with our weapons. Still no snake appeared.

"Look," I said. "We don't know where the snake is but it knows exactly where we are so let's get out of here. Let's go sleep outside. We can sleep on the lumber pile."

"Maybe the snake is gone."

"Maybe it is," I replied. "But what if it isn't? I'm not getting back into my bed tonight. Do you really want to sleep here in the house?"

"No. OK, let's go out."

We divided Brehane's blankets, went out into the night, and found spaces on the lumber pile. The moon was out, the stars were bright, the night insects dramatic. This wasn't so bad. We settled in the for the night.

Suddenly, we heard a cry from the far edge of the village. "Lion, lion whoooo!"

This warning was repeated a couple of times by other, closer voices as the lion passed deeper into the village, heading our way.

"Are you really sure about the snake in your bed?"

"I'm sure." Actually, I was only about 85% sure by this time but that's pretty sure and there was no way I was going to crawl back into my bed in the dark.

In a few moments we could hear the breathing of the lion. It was getting close. We both tried to suppress our own breathing. That worked well but my heartbeat must have been audible as far away as the river, maybe the next village.

Soon the lion was right there. We could hear it pacing and breathing heavily. It was in the brush between my house and Banjaw's. Then suddenly it was running. Our way. It turned slightly, cut between the lumber pile and my latrine, and tore into the thorny brush corral at Zemanuel's house only fifteen meters away.

A major uproar ensued. We could hear the lion snarling, the cows bellowing, the corral coming apart, and shouting from all the houses nearby. Soon there were torches and flashlights in the night, converging on the corral. Cattle began rushing around us in a panic, banging into and disrupting both sides of our lumber pile.

The lion sounded equally frantic, brushing against our lumber pile as it raced past us in the night. It caught a cow coming around the corner of my house and quickly dispatched it. But the carcass was too big for the lion to haul away and the lights and shouting were too much so the lion took its leave, headed back west toward the wall of the valley. Meanwhile, we could hear the whooping of hyenas in the forest. What a thrill for them - cows were rushing to meet them in the woods, at night.

Brehane and I were still on the lumber pile, now sitting up, wide awake, and a thought struck me - in a few weeks I'd be in another place, where a night like this would be unimaginable, maybe unbelievable, and it seemed funny and I began to laugh, quietly I thought.

"What are you laughing at?" Brehane asked.

No answer occurred to me that I thought would would make sense to him. "This is just so crazy," I finally managed. "This night."

There was a pause. "You're crazy."

"Maybe so," I conceded. I could hear him laugh at that and we called it a night, wrapped ourselves in our blankets, and spent the rest of the night on the lumber pile.

It turned out that the cow killed at the corner of my house was Getachew's and, following Merhabete custom, the farmers and their wives gathered early the next morning to buy portions of the meat at a low price. This tradition, virtually always honored, cushioned the impact on Getachew of losing a cow and provided meat that was affordable to those who might otherwise find meat beyond their budgets. The other cattle that had charged into the forest that night were lucky or wily enough to have avoided fatal hyena encounters.

I bought a nice piece of meat and, as I often did on market day, passed it over to Tamtim and Kedist, who cooked beef like nobody else, cooked it until it was soft as butter and we shared it by the light of the cooking fire. Then, as he often did, Tamtim went out and got some honey-comb from his hive for dessert and we sat on the log that served as a bench in their house, munching quietly and in profound contentment, honey dripping onto our chins. And I thought, can life be more pleasant than this? It was one of the last evenings I spent with them before departing Wajifo for good. We had a good laugh over the snake and lion adventure of the night before and I swore I'd keep fresh batteries on hand for the rest of my life.

SAVAGES

It was not until my fourth year in Ethiopia, returning from
a trip to Sodo, that I was warned of savages in Gemu Gofa.

I had collected my mail, bought a few things, got on the bus
and was in my seat, daydreaming, waiting for the bus to
depart. A young Ethiopian Naval officer sat down next to
me, introduced himself, and we struck up a conversation as
the bus rolled south toward Wajifo.

He asked where I was going. I told him Wajifo.

"Where is that?"

"It's in Gemu Gofa. It's a small village north of Arba
Minch."

"Well, I myself, I'm going to Arba Minch today and then,
from there, I'll have to figure out where to go next. I'm on
leave and I decided to go see the savages in Gemu Gofa."

"What?" I said. The savages?"

"Yes, the savages. I understand that most of the people in
Gemu Gofa are savages. Many of them are cannibals."

"That hasn't been my experience."

188

"Really? I understand that they're everywhere. You really need to be careful."

"Well, the people I live with are mostly farmers and their wives, and a few teachers."

"They may want you to think that's what they are but I'm certain some of them would eat you if they had the chance. You don't know our country the way I do."

"I'm sure that's true."

"Yes. Be very careful. Don't trust them, they can turn on you without warning."

I tried to picture Asfaw biting my arm and smiled. "I have quite a few friends in Wajifo," I said. "None of them are cannibals or what I would consider a savage."

"I'm just saying you can't trust these people," he responded patiently if a bit condescendingly. "I've heard all about them."

His advice was almost too silly to cause offence but was not quite hilarious either given the consequences of the urban elite's casual contempt for the rural poor.

I steered the conversation in other directions. He proved a pleasant conversationalist, the time went by quickly, and before long, it seemed, we were at the river, the northern border of Wajifo.

The river was up, at flood stage, dark brown, and charging angrily toward the lake. There was no way to get across so everyone got out of the bus to view the spectacle. After a while we could see people gathering on the far shore as well. The roar of the flood was too loud for us to hear the shouts of those on the other side but I could see Asfaw, Getachew, Tamtim and a few others. They saw me too and we waved our arms slowly over our heads in greeting.

After half an hour or so the river had dropped enough to consider trying to wade across, and my friends on the opposite bank signaled me to do so. They started in themselves, holding hands to form a chain and proceeding with caution.

I waited a few more minutes since I had nothing to cling to for support and then waded in, tentatively. I was on the relatively shallow side of the river, about knee high. My friends had to cross the main channel.

"What are you doing?" the Naval officer demanded. "You don't know who those people are. They could be savages. Cannibals. You should wait for the bus."

"No," I said, carefully turning around to face him. "There are no cannibals here. These are friends of mine. I live here. They're coming over to help me get across."

Then I turned my back on him and concentrated on keeping my balance in the still swiftly moving river. In a few minutes I reached Asfaw in the middle of the river, just at the edge of the main channel, which I would not have considered trying to cross by myself.

I passed one of my two bundles to Asfaw who passed it on to Tamtim and he on to Getachew and the others, and so on across the channel and back to the river bank, a bluff at this point. Then the same with the other bundle.

Meanwhile, we could hear the Naval officer calling to me. "Be careful!" he yelled. "Be careful."

I didn't respond and the chain my friends had formed began to pull back, pulling me with them to the safety of the high river bank.

We sat on the bluff, resting, watching the river. Soon we could see the passengers get back on the bus and the bus make its own careful way across the river, downstream from where we sat.

Getachew turned to me. "Who was that man yelling at you? What was he saying? He was speaking your language wasn't he? I couldn't understand him."

191

"He was just someone I met on the bus. And yes, he was speaking English."

"What was he yelling?"

"He was saying that I should be careful."

"Well, that was good advice but you were safe. We had you at the deep part."

"We had you," repeated Tamtim absently.

I looked at them, sitting there, wet and tired.

"Yes, you did. You had me. I knew I was safe. Thanks."

Getachew slowly, carefully got to his feet and stretched.

"Let's go find some *tela*," he said.

MY FRIENDS

My departure date was approaching. Brehane would need a place to live since my house was, officially, the community development center. So we built a house for him with the help of one of the Merhabete farmers. It was framed with eucalyptus poles, the gaps filled with tree branches, and the inside covered with bamboo matting. The floor was dirt and the roof was tin, just like my house but a bit smaller.

We moved the chicken coops and all the chickens over to his place, along with the rabbit hutch. We dug a latrine. I divided my tools between Brehane and Tamtim, and gave my desk and books to Habtu, who was interested in everything.

Getachew was over at my place as I was dividing things up and packing for my departure. We drank tea and talked. As he prepared to go I said, "Getachew, you always use the same cup for your tea at my place. Why don't you take it? In fact, it's yours. Take it with you."

"Really?"

"Yes."

"Thank you. I really like this cup."

And so it went with a few other items – my shelves to Bogali, my mirror to Tesfaye, and so forth.

I would need to send money to Brehane so we set up a bank account in Sodo and deposited enough money to hold him over for a few months until I could get settled back in the U.S. We got him a post office box.

Mengistu came by near the end and we had our first real conversation in months.

"What happened?" he asked me. "We used to be close friends, brothers, and now we hardly see each other. Bekelech is gone. Our son died. I'm not really a farmer anymore." He lit a cigarette. "I smoke these things now. I drink too much. Everything is different."

I had no answer except that the pressure of just trying to survive in an unjust world, the unfair resolution of his land dispute, the dishonesty and corruption of the government, all these things had changed his life and fortune. I said that I thought Bekelech understood that but I was sure that he had been hard for her to live with. Even I had found him hard to be around, although I sympathized with him. I was sure he knew that.

I reminded him that with coaching from Bernard, he had operated a cement mixer while working on an irrigation project not long before. He had had no earlier experience operating machinery of any kind yet took to it like it was his profession.

"You're smart," I told him. "You can read now and operate machinery or learn to very quickly. Maybe you should get out of Wajifo and see what kind of work you can find. Anyway, I don't blame you for anything and I hope you don't blame me. I wish you a good life."

Suddenly, unexpectedly he began crying, sobbing. I didn't know what to do so I made some tea and waited him out, trying a few times to say something supportive but each time I did he waved me off. It was as if he had to do this and then he'd be alright. He finally stopped, caught his breath, swallowed his tea, and stood up to leave. I stood too. Then, without saying another word, he embraced me and walked out the door, heading toward the marketplace.

Habtu and I had a couple of long conversations about the future. We both felt that the military would be taking over the government before long and that Ethiopia would probably have a leftist military government for the next twenty years or so. I felt that such governments are usually not friendly to the United States and so, depending on how militant the revolutionary government turned out to be, it was unlikely that I would see him in the foreseeable future. But I hoped to one day.

The last couple of days I walked around the village saying my goodbyes. Then one morning I simply got up, headed out to the road, and caught the bus to Addis Abeba.

I had eight hours of travel ahead of me before I'd arrive in the capital city and it seemed only minutes after we'd crossed the river that thoughts began to bubble up of their own accord. Memories raced through my mind as fragments, snapshots of shared meals, friends lost, snakes, lions, and episodes of elation, frustration, and illness.

Unbidden and without the perspective that time and distance can bring, I found myself undertaking an informal and rather scattered account of my four years in Wajifo, hoping that I'd made a significant difference. I leaned my head back and let the thoughts come.

I felt satisfied that I had met my commitment to Kebede and Bahylu to take care of their younger brother and had arranged things so that I could continue to support him from the U.S. This seemed especially important because they had both died since our agreement had been reached.

I felt tired, which wasn't surprising since I'd contracted malaria and hepatitis among numerous cases of viral illnesses over the years, tested positive for tuberculosis, and harbored a calcification on my lung, all while hosting the intestinal parasites I had welcomed upon my arrival. Unbeknownst to me at the time, the profound fatigue I was experiencing was caused by liver damage, a side effect of the drug the Peace Corps doctor had prescribed to treat my tuberculosis, a drug which should not have been prescribed due to my history of hepatitis.

Perhaps because of my own compromised health, I felt especially thankful for the many times I had been able to treat wounds, infections and other health problems, not through any formal program but simply because people in

196

need came to my door. I'd kept a supply of ointments, antibiotics, bandages, and other materials on hand so that I could be helpful. To relieve pain in another, even at the micro level, is immensely rewarding.

I felt grateful for the countless times the people of Wajifo had helped me and made me feel welcome. I thought of Aserati putting his life on the line to save me from the snake in my rabbit hutch. Had I thanked him enough? Could I ever? I thought of how Habtu had helped me continue the adult literacy classes after our use of the school was denied. His energy and commitment making the project not only effective but fun. I hoped it would have a lasting impact on the lives of the Wajifo farmers.

I felt hopeful that endeavors like the chicken breeds and improved seeds for cash crops I'd introduced, and a cotton marketing coop I'd organized with Kebede and Tamtim would prove fruitful for my friends and neighbors for years to come. But the truth was that none of these projects would have been possible without the cooperation and commitment of the Wajifo farmers. Kebede had been such a steady hand and reliable friend, a natural leader and a good man. I felt his loss deeply. I knew I would also miss the calm, gentle friendship of Tamtim and Kedist, and sitting around the cooking fire with Bogali talking about religion, moon landings or just the events of the day.

I hoped Bekelech had landed in a safe place and that Mengistu's life would turn in a positive direction, despite the odds against that.

I smiled to myself as I thought of my efforts to promote the use of latrines. While they were at least marginally embraced by the villagers, in nearly every case the farmer requesting help said he was building the latrine for his wife. I thought of the strange looks I received when I managed to truck several dozen discarded metal barrels from Addis Abeba to use as rain barrels for the houses with tin roofs and rat-proof grain storage bins for the homes with thatch roofs. Luckily, they worked.

I dozed off and then, suddenly, the bus was pulling into the dusty terminal in Addis Abba.

Habtu and Brehane had wanted to see me off at the airport, but I knew that there would be administrative things to attend to in the Peace Corps office so we arranged to meet in the city a few days later. It was very good to see them and we spent a couple of pleasant though melancholy days together. But my travel arrangements took longer than expected and they had to get back to Wajifo, so I ended up seeing them off at the bus terminal instead. This was hard and sad but I was feeling strangely numb and so got through it without causing a scene.

That evening though, at a friend's house, the night before my flight to the United States, I was reflecting during dinner on how, four years earlier, I had decided that I wanted to understand what it was like to be a peasant farmer in Ethiopia. What it was like for most people to experience life throughout human history. To grasp the true human condition.

I excused myself and found a back room, closed the door behind me and let my numbness just melt away. I cried like Mengistu had.

I cried for the injustices faced by the people I had come to know in Wajifo. Those people. Their hard lives. The odds against them. The contempt they endured. Their eternal optimism, their tenacity, their bravery. And their friendship. My friends.

EPILOGUE

Twenty-five years after leaving Ethiopia, I was in Uganda on business. Before leaving home I had reflected on the fact that this was as close to Ethiopia as I was likely to be for some time, maybe forever. So I got a visa at the Ethiopian consulate in Washington and bought a ticket. My time in Uganda was not exactly wasted but I was distracted, thinking of Ethiopia and especially of Wajifo.

I had managed to keep in touch with Brehane for a little while, sending him money and exchanging occasional letters. And with Habtu as well, and through them with a few others in the community. This had worked well for about three years but as the hard core Marxist government that had replaced the emperor, became more oppressive and suspicious it began to seem dangerous for my friends to be receiving letters from the U.S. and especially dangerous for Brehane to be the regular recipient of money from there.

The news from Ethiopia carried reports of a student being executed for having American money in his pocket at a government checkpoint. Then an Ethiopian employee of an American humanitarian organization was shot dead on the street in Arba Minch simply because of his employment.

I consulted with an old friend, Marc Scott, who I knew from my Peace Corps days and who had recently been working in Ethiopia, about what to do.

"I would stop writing and stop sending money immediately," he advised. "You could really get someone in trouble, maybe get someone killed."

"OK, I'll send one last letter telling them that I think it's wise to stop communicating, and that Brehane should expect no more financial support."

"No. Just stop communicating. That letter could be the one that gets someone killed."

So, without warning or explanation, I stopped communicating with my friends. And soon afterward stopped hearing from them. I hoped but couldn't know that this was because they had come to the same conclusion I had. So, when I finally went back it had been about twenty-two years since I had stopped writing.

I hired a car and driver in Addis Abeba and headed south, tingling with anticipation.

Wajifo was much bigger than the village I had left. There had been resettlement programs under the Marxists that had changed the ethnic flavor of the village, the appearance of its people. It wasn't just Merhabete and Gemu anymore. At first I saw no Merhabete at all. Then someone who had been a student when I'd been there recognized me and steered me to the home of Goshu, one of my old Merhabete neighbors, a farmer I remembered for his generosity, easy-going nature, infectious laugh, and for his interest in cross breeding chickens. He had gone gray but otherwise was his old self.

Our reunion was emotional for us both, and soon I was surrounded by Merhabete I had known or their children, the parents having passed away. I spent the day responding to invitations for coffee. With Tamtim and Kedist's recently orphaned daughter, born after I had left. With Tesfaye who had married Getachew's sister, had a little family, and still sported the dent in his temple bestowed by Mulugeta many years ago. And with many others until I simply could not absorb any more caffeine.

Getachew had died, killed in the war with Eritrea that he had been drafted into.

Getachew's sister fetched a cup from a wooden chest, and asked, "Does this look familiar?"

It did, a bit anyway. "Yes, it does. What is it?"

"This is the cup you gave to Getachew when you left. He called it 'Ye bill tasa' (Bill's cup) and would tell stories about you, conversations you had. Would you like to hold it?"

The honest answer would have been no. I was filled with emotion, seeping tears all day, and was trying to maintain some composure, but I reached out and took it. I remembered handing it to Getachew at the end of my time in Wajifo. I had a flood of memories while I tried not to imagine his death on some pointless battlefield in the north.

The day was filled with similar encounters. I sent a message to Asfaw in Arba Minch, hoping he could come up the next day.

I was surprised and pleased to see some Leghorn chickens pecking for bugs and grass and a huge, self-important Anak rooster strutting about Goshu's house. "Remember these?" he smiled.

The Merhabete killed a goat and cooked it for dinner, and I had the experience I had missed and wanted most to experience again. We sat on logs or homemade benches, on the dirt floor, near the cooking fire, sharing injera and the goat meat, surrounded by friends and the children of friends, the flickering firelight reflecting off all those familiar, if aged faces, the low murmur of Amharic conversation. We told stories of things we remembered from those days – funny things, sad things, projects that we'd worked on together.

When dinner was finished I said I wanted to explain something to them, something that had bothered me for many years.

"Speak! Speak!"

It felt right to stand up. Then, with the help of the hired driver because my Amharic had grown rusty and I wanted to get this right, I explained why I had stopped writing. I had hated to do that, I said, but it seemed like the safest thing to do. I was afraid they would think I had forgotten them and I was there, that night, to assure them that I had never forgotten them and that I thought of them almost every day. And that this, this meal, right there, that night, eating with all of them was one of the best experiences of my life. And I meant it.

Abera then stood up and thanked me for all that he felt I had contributed to the community, that being an educated foreigner it was especially remarkable. He remembered meeting me for the first time when we were moving heavy sacks of cement from a storage site to a project and he was amazed that I actually carried those heavy loads on my back. No other educated man, no one who worked for the government would ever do such a thing. And, he finished, "It means more to us here than I have the words to express that you have come back to see us once again."

Eventually, it was time to call it a night. I said goodnight to everyone as they left, receiving and giving hugs and kisses and expressions of gratitude. Goshu insisted that I take his bed and that he sleep on a wooden bench. I drifted off to sleep with the once-familiar sound of the insects drowning out all others, except for the whoop of a hyena which felt like a welcome home.

The next morning, I hiked up the river to my favorite bathing spot. Later, I reconnected with Asfaw who had gotten my note and come up from Arba Minch by bus. We chatted for a couple of hours until it was time for me to head back north.

I'd learned that Brehane was working as a day laborer at a hospital in a town about half way to Addis Abeba. We stopped there and I found him living under very difficult conditions and with five children to feed. We opened up a bank account in his name and I gave him whatever money I had on me that I could spare. We spent the night talking until we both fell asleep. We found coffee in the morning and I was on my way again.

Once back in Addis Abeba I was able to track down Habtu by phone. He said he was in the north, working on an agricultural project to help poor farmers.

Mengistu, who I had really hoped to see, was out in eastern Ethiopia working as a tractor driver. The Wajifo farmers told me he was making good money.

I was able to keep in touch with Habtu, Asfaw, and Brehane for a while before eventually, and perhaps inevitably, losing contact again.

But my memories and, I like to think, those friendships live on.

ACKNOWLEDGEMENTS

This memoir is much better than it would have been if not for the questions, suggestions, and encouragement of family and friends.

Some of the most detailed sets of comments I received are not actually reflected in the final draft, although not because I didn't value them. I did. Frequently they made me think more critically about my story. What was I trying to accomplish? Ultimately, however, I decided that I was being encouraged to write an economic development piece or an Ethiopian history book, or some other project. This realization helped me focus more precisely on the book that I actually wanted to write. At any rate, whether I accepted an editorial suggestion or not, I deeply appreciate the generosity of all those who read drafts and provided me with critical comments of any sort.

Most of all I must express my profound gratitude to my daughter Abby who read every draft and offered outstanding editorial comments and criticisms at every step of the way, meanwhile writing her own book.

My wife Leslie encouraged me for years to get started on this book and, once underway, to finish it. Her enthusiasm for the project helped me keep going when my own motivation occasionally waned.

And a special thank you to Joanne Lozar Glenn, my creative nonfiction teacher, who encouraged me to press on and write more when I had only written one story and thought I was finished.

Beyond that, I would like to thank Jody Sugrue for designing the cover and Lew Mermelstein for permission to use his photos. Thanks to Molly and Mandy Sugrue, Fred and Mary Ginsberg, Tom and Ed Sugrue, Ann Granger, Rich DeGennaro, Tom Stanley, George Taylor, and Wyn Cooper for their comments, suggestions, and support.

I am deeply indebted to Mike Pusey for his guidance in bringing the book to publication.

And a sincere thank you to everyone who said, "Tell me when your book is ready. I'd love to read it." When I got bogged down those comments helped keep me going.

THE AUTHOR:

Bill Sugrue spent thirty years working in the foreign aid
program of the United States, focusing especially on the
intersection of environment, natural resource management,
and social justice. In addition to his years in Ethiopia, he
served long-term residencies in Haiti, Peru, and Guatemala
as well as in Washington, D.C. with dozens of short-term
assignments in Asia, Africa, Central and South America. He
retired as a Senior Foreign Service Officer in the United
States Agency for International Development.

76040270R00133

Made in the USA
Columbia, SC
22 September 2019